SPHERE COLOUR PLANT GUIDES
HOUSE PLANTS

D1375032

SPHERE

SPHERE BOOKS LIMITED

30-32 Gray's Inn Road, London WCIX 8JL

CONTENTS

INTRODUCTION

It is far easier to grow successful house plants these days than it was twenty or thirty years ago. Not only are there many more varieties, of a far greater quality, but nowadays the knowledge of plants and their care is available to everyone.

Anyone who wants to grow house plants and is prepared to devote the necessary time and care to them will soon develop 'green fingers' – that instinctive touch required for successful gardening.

But the increase in the number of plant varieties available also has its disadvantages. It is relatively easy to grow just, say, geraniums or begonias year in year out. After a while you know exactly what is good for them, the spot in your home where they grow best and how to take cuttings etc. But there are hundreds of different plant varieties. Some need more light than others, some need plenty of water, others only a little, and many of them need a regular dose of plant food.

In order to know exactly what is good for each of these plants you would need to be a professor of horticulture – and that rules most of us out. This is why it is such a good thing that there are so many books on the subject so that we can learn all we need to know about plant care. If you wished you could fill whole bookcases with books on house plants but if you tried to read them all you would have no time left to care for your plants.

This is why we thought it would be useful to lay down a few basic details, knowledge of which is essential for successful care of house plants, and to set them out in as few words as possible in an easy reference guide.

Among the basic, but vital, information you need to know are things like where best to stand your plant, what temperature suits it and how to feed it. Information like this is vital to the health of plants.

4

We have attempted to provide a condensed handbook which gives as much information on the subject as possible. On pages 34-73 you will find essential guidelines for the care of roughly 240 varieties. In the short description under the pictures you will find details concerning the flowering season, temperature, the necessary amount of water, the best place to stand each plant, feeding, propagation and re-potting. The 240 plants are listed alphabetically under their Latin names. If you want to look up the English names consult the register on pages 94 to 96. There you will find the English name with the corresponding Latin name of the plant about which you want to read.

This little guide book also contains short chapters on the subject of hydroculture, plant diseases and how to cure them, the best re-potting technique and why pruning is neccessary and how best to do it.

Plant-lovers will find these tips very useful but there is one thing that nobody can teach you and that is the love of plants. A plant is like a child, it needs love, attention and patience. Lavish these on your plants and you will be delighted with the pleasure you get in return.

HOUSE PLANTS GALORE

If you have already glanced through this booklet you will have seen some of the 240 house plants illustrated from page 34 onwards. There are considerably more than you could comfortably fit into your home, so how do you decide which ones to buy?

In practice this is not quite as difficult as it may seem. There are many breeds of dogs and people usually manage to pick the one for which they are best suited and it is the same with house plants.

Firstly consider your personal circumstances. If you live in a rather dark house with few windows you would be wise to choose a plant which does not need a vast amount of light, e.g. *Chamaedorea* (see page 43) or *Howeia Kentia* (see page 60). It is, of course, possible to provide plants which stand in a dark corner with artificial light.

If you live in a small house you will obviously choose plants which do not take up excessive space. In any event your personal taste is bound to play a decisive role. There are plants which flower abundantly and others which are evergreens.
There are standing, hanging, climbing and creeping plants. There are plants with large multi-coloured leaves and then there are plants with fine, delicate foliage.

Plants are a highly personal matter and your own character and temperament can often be a more important factor in your choice than you realise. There are plants which need a great deal of attention and others which are very easy-going and which don't mind being neglect-

Begonia rex has beautifully coloured leaves. Scirpus, a quill-wort variety, in bloom.

WHICH ONES SHALL WE CHOOSE?

ed occasionally, for a day or two. In deciding which plants to buy you would do well to decide what sort of a person you are and how well you will be able to look after the plants.

If you feel you won't be able to give your plants a great deal of attention and are looking for varieties which won't mind being forgotten once in a while you would do well to choose plants such as *Chlorophytum, Cissus, Cyperus, Fatshedera, Philodendron, Sansevieria* or *Tradescantia,* just to mention a few of the tougher varieties. It is obvious that these resistant types are best suited, for instance, to offices and other places of work where they may not always be tended with clockwork regularity.

All these criteria help us to decide what variety of house plant we will buy. Another very important factor is placing the plant in the right position. Neither you nor your plant are going to be very happy if you make a wrong choice here. For instance, if you have a valuable piece of furniture you won't want to place a plant upon it which needs regular spraying. On the following pages you will find some suggestions concerning the choice of suitable plants for the various rooms in your home.

There is a strong temptation to place your house plants on items of furniture like tables and bookcases. This can look very attractive but there are a number of drawbacks especially if the furniture is made from wood or wood veneer. Spraying or watering the plants can leave unsightly smears on the wood. There is also the problem that,

The Ficus elastica is a rewarding type of house plant, just like the Dracaena marginata (right). The Ficus is fundamentally a fig tree and likes half-shade. Dracaena can take more light. Both plants, however, are of tropical origin, although they come from different parts of the world, so both can stand considerable heat. See care instructions in the Glossary (pages 34-73).

since your plants need light, you will stand the furniture which carries the plants in a direct light source. This can harm the wood. Plants do not like to be moved around a lot and for both the reasons mentioned we would advise choosing a permanent spot on a window sill, a ledge or a shelf. Always remember that your plant will grow, in some cases quite a lot. When selecting your spot make sure that it will still be suitable for the plant in the months and years to come. Climbing plants need firm supports or trellises. Weak supports can sometimes be pulled down as the plant climbs which can in turn lead to the plant collapsing.

Fatshedera is a cross between Fatsia japonica and ivy.

Some people are allergic to some pot plants. The *Primula obconica*, for instance, can give a nasty itchy rash. *Streptocarpus* (Cape primrose) can have a similar effect.

House plants can be a considerable investment and to make sure that you are giving them the best care possible check the tips on page 78. These will explain what to do for instance if your leaves turn yellow or brown.

Climbing plants need gentle support.

The section on pruning will explain how to see that your plant grows and develops best and a further section, on taking cuttings, will show you how to use the prunings from your plants to grow entirely new ones. In short, having house plants is

Neoregelia, or nest-bromelia as it is sometimes called. It has no objection to being watered in the centre of its leaves but, be sure to use luke-warm water!

Rhipsalidopsis, or Easter Cactus can flower abundantly in Spring.

not just a pleasant way of decorating your home, it is a fascinating and absorbing experience with nature.

House plants have become very popular in recent years but they are still not as popular as in other countries, particularly America and Holland. Over there the house plant market is vast and the majority of homes have quite a collection. Walk down a residential street in Holland and you will see house plants used to form a screen instead of curtains. Go into a home in most parts of America and you will find an abundance of plants – so much so that hanging baskets now provide the only new area of space not yet filled with foliage.

House plants come in very many shapes and sizes. Some are expensive and difficult to take care of but there is a wide variety of plants which are both relatively inexpensive and which produce a colourful foliage.

WHERE SHALL WE STAND THE PLANT?

Let's assume that you've bought a plant – or better still, that you have been given one as a present. Where should you stand it? Not every spot in your home is suitable for growing plants and in order to grow them successfully it is necessary to comply with certain basic requirements. If your plant is to feel at home there must be enough light, sufficient humidity and the temperature must be right. These three factors, light, humidity and temperature are the 'big three' in successful plant growing and should always be taken into consideration when deciding where to place your plant.

Always remember, however, that if your plants stand close to the window you should make sure they are not in bright sunlight for too long. The majority of plants do not like direct sunlight. Another problem associated with plants on window sills comes if they are near the window pane. The difference in temperature, especially in winter, between the outside and the inside is tremendous and on one side the plant will benefit from the warmth of the room while on the other it will be getting the cold radiated through the glass. You wouldn't lean up against the window for long so why make your plant suffer?

Plants lend atmosphere to any home.

LIGHT

Although house plants are mostly grown in nurseries nowadays this does not mean that their basic growing habits have changed. In their natural surroundings they need light and it is therefore no more than simple logic that you should ensure that your house plants get a sufficient supply. Light is vital to your house plants if they are to grow and develop in the way they should. Stand them in too dark a place and they will slowly deteriorate. Place them on a window sill or near a window and they will reward you by growing healthily. This is also why plants grow better against a light coloured wall, and suffer when they are placed up against a wall with a dark covering. If your plants must be placed in a dark spot this problem can be overcome with the use of artificial light. The best method of supplying artificial light is by the use of fluorescent tubes. Plants can also thrive if they are placed in a spot which provides reflected light from another room. Careful positioning can ensure that even in a room without a direct light source your plants can get enough reflected light to grow properly.

Special lamps can help plants to grow sturdy and straight.

TEMPERATURE

House plants which we grow in our homes may have come from a nursery but they originate in places with much warmer climates than our own. Plants like the African violet and the desert cactus are used to plenty of heat and could not survive for very long if placed out in our gardens.

They require an even temperature in our homes and there are a number of places in the house, like the hall, where the constant and often dramatic temperature changes will do them harm. Every time the front door is open cold air flows in, while heat from the hall radiator flows out. This sort of fluctuating temperature is quite unsuitable. We repeat, because it is vital, an even temperature is very important. In Summer it should be five to ten degrees warmer than in Winter.

Where possible we have indicated the ideal temperature for the plants illustrated on pages 34-73.

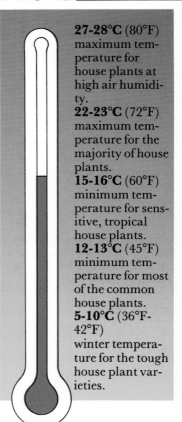

27-28°C (80°F) maximum temperature for house plants at high air humidity.
22-23°C (72°F) maximum temperature for the majority of house plants.
15-16°C (60°F) minimum temperature for sensitive, tropical house plants.
12-13°C (45°F) minimum temperature for most of the common house plants.
5-10°C (36°F-42°F) winter temperature for the tough house plant varieties.

Orchids are becoming increasingly popular as house plants. Most varieties originate in the rain forests of South America or Asia. However, it is possible to grow certain types in your home. Check with your supplier.

HUMIDITY

Plants need water. The food which they require for growth and development is found in the water sucked up by their roots. If you water the soil in the pot with relatively sterile tap water then the organic elements contained in the compost are gradually dissolved and it is precisely these elements which the plants require in order to thrive.

After a while the soil becomes poor and drained of its richness. This is why it is advisable to give your plants extra food at regular intervals – once a week or once a fortnight as indicated in our plant care guide – in the form of plant food added to the water.

There are various types of plant food available. With these always follow the manufacturers instructions.

Rain water is better for your plants than tap water, as it contains quite a number of nutrient elements.

Wherever possible it is therefore best to spray your plants with rain water. Not only is it better for them but it is softer and reduces the chances of getting unsightly chalk marks on the leaves. These chalk marks, which result from spraying, are unsightly but easy to remove with any of the 'leafshine' products available in spray or tube form. (If in tube form simply dissolve a small quantity of the product in water and sponge the leaves with the solution, they will take on a beautiful, healthy sheen). Spraying is very important for your plants especially in winter when the atmosphere can become very dry from heating systems. Your plants need vapour and water finely distributed between the leaves. Too much water can cause damage but a fine shower from a plant spray can never do any harm.

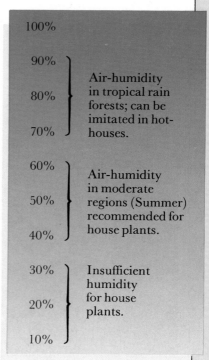

100%

90%
80% } Air-humidity in tropical rain forests; can be imitated in hot-houses.
70%

60%
50% } Air-humidity in moderate regions (Summer) recommended for house plants.
40%

30%
20% } Insufficient humidity for house plants.
10%

THE LIVING AND DINING-ROOM

What a difference plants can make to our homes. Take a look at this photograph... How much less attractive this room would be without the plants.

There is always something happening with plants – a new bud emerges, a plant turns towards the light, leaves change colour. All this provides a constant source of interest and every new development subtly changes the surroundings in your room.

Plants in living rooms and dining rooms enrich our lives and practically all types of house plants are suitable for the living room. Always bear in mind, though, the 'big three' factors of light, temperature and humidity and always choose a draught-free spot.

THE KITCHEN

For some the kitchen is simply a place of work in which to spend as little time as possible. For others it is a room with atmosphere and is used not only for cooking but as a focal point of the home.

Herbs are splendid things to grow in your kitchen. They will benefit your cooking and add to the look of the room. Grow them on the window sill and start with varieties which are easy to grow like thyme, parsley, rosemary, chives and even garlic. Most of them can be grown from seed and will give a tang to your cooking that dried herbs cannot match.

THE CONSERVATORY

If you have a conservatory or greenhouse attached to your home both you and your house plants are very fortunate. A good old-fashioned conservatory – a built-out construction with lots of glass – or an attached greenhouse into which you can walk, provides ideal surroundings for your plants.

They get light from several sides, few plants can thrive, in hot, direct sunlight. Out of doors they are used to it but indoors the sunlight must be filtered without taking away too much light, and the conservatory or greenhouse provides the perfect answer. Be careful to avoid draughts and try to keep the atmosphere as damp as possible by spraying and by putting a bowl of water in places where it can evaporate easily. All plants, with the rare exception of those that like the shade, will thrive in your conservatory or greenhouse.

THE BATHROOM

Given sufficient room and light the bathroom can prove an ideal place for plants. Once again, however, there are rules to remember.

First, and foremost, make sure that you choose plants which can withstand fairly dramatic changes in temperature. Most plants are not suited to this and will soon wilt under the strain. Air humidity will also fluctuate and, if you regularly open the window after your bath, there will be cold draughts. All these factors make it extremely important that you select a hardy variety of house plant.

Secondly, house plants do not react well to doses of talcum powder and aerosol spray so watch how you use them. Finally, don't put too many plants in the bathroom. You don't want to have to climb through a jungle to take a bath and they do not react well if people are constantly brushing up against then.

Asparagus sprengeri (Asparagus Fern), can live happily in a bath-room but beware of its prickly foliage.

THE GREEN BEDROOM

Some people find the idea of having plants in the bedroom a bit odd.

'I only go there at night and even then I spend most of the time with my eyes shut' is a frequent reaction.

However, there is no reason at all why you shouldn't grow plants in your bedroom – as long as you treat them properly – and even the sceptics will find that this adds a new and refreshing dimension.

It is important to remember a few ground rules, not the least of which is to put them well out of the way. Stand them in a corner, hang them from the wall in baskets or put them on the window sill.

Another danger that comes from having plants in your bedroom is that, since most bedrooms are upstairs, they tend to be neglected. It is easy and quick to go around the ground floor of your home spraying your plants but some people tend to forget the ones which are upstairs.

If you fear that you may neglect plants in your bedroom why not place a bottle garden there. This will give you all the benefits that come from having plants in a bedroom and it will largely take care of itself.

THE OFFICE

In the nineteenth century, offices and workrooms were dark, dreary, dusty places. It is only in the last ten to twenty years that people have realised the importance of having a light and cheerful working environment. This not only promotes greater efficiency at work, but also keeps people in a far better humour.

Well lit rooms are ideal for house plants. If you arrange with your colleagues that the plants are watered and checked twice a week they will thrive. Make your place of work as pleasant as possible; plants can play an important role where this is concerned.

Since we always buy our house plants in potting compost it is easy to assume that they will not grow in anything else. Good compost does contain all the elements required to produce healthy plants. It gives the necessary support to the roots and anchors the plant firmly. The loam contains nutrients and oxygen and it is easy to supply the moisture which carries those nutrients through to the roots.

These are all definite advantages but there are also certain disadvantages. In a flowerpot filled with compost the roots have relatively little room to grow and can become potbound. A flowerpot also contains only a fixed amount of compost and after a while the nutritious elements in it become exhausted.

This is why plants need re-potting from time to time. The object of hydroculture is to capitalise on the advantages of compost while eliminating its disadvantages. Instead of rooting in normal compost the plants are usually rooted in hard, baked clay pellets. These provide the same anchoring as normal compost and are also very light and absorbent and can soak up 25% of their weight in water. Hydroculture requires special pots which consist of two parts. The outer part is a simple cylindrical pot while the inner part has openings in the side and bottom. Attached to the pot is a water-level indicator. Before planting, roots must be washed in lukewarm water until they are absolutely clean. There must not be a single grain of earth either on or between the roots. Next, pour a layer of pellets to a depth of three or four centimetres into the inner pot. Then hold the plant with its roots in the pot and pour in more

Carefully remove all the earth from the roots.

Place the plant in the inner pot and fill with clay pellets.

Place the inner pot in the outer pot and check the water level.

pellets until it is firmly positioned. Flush the pot thoroughly with luke-warm water – this sets the clay pellets firmly between the roots and anchors the plant. Next place the inner pot into the outer pot and pour in water to the required level. The roots will then hang free in the water. Check the water level regularly. During the first week just add water whenever the indicator shows it is necessary. After a week the plant must be given food as well since the clay pellets contain no nutrients. Special soluble tablets can be bought for this purpose or, alternatively, use plant food. Always follow the dosage specified on the packet or bottle.

The water will need to be changed roughly once every six weeks since plants do not grow well in stagnant water. Hydroculture is not very expensive but you do need to buy these special pots.

A GARDEN IN A BOTTLE

Nowadays the most popular jars for bottle gardens are those wide-necked green ones available in garden centres, supermarkets and florists. Just as satisfactory, but rarer, are the ones once used for storing acid. Both types are ideal 'incubators' for house plants, and more and more people are turning to them to provide miniature 'greenhouses'.

These jars offer perfect conditions for growing your house plants – they are beautifully protected from draughts, smoke and other pollution in the air, they don't dry out and are shielded from sudden changes of temperature. The atmosphere inside the jars is very well balanced and in order to maintain that balance they should not be placed in direct sunlight but should stand where they can get plenty of light. Because of this balance your bottle garden will hardly ever need watering. A small amount of water sprayed on the plants every six months or so will be quite sufficient.

Filling the bottle is not as difficult as you might imagine. Before you start wash it very thoroughly, especially if it has had acid in it, and dry it out well. Place a layer of gravel a few centimetres thick on the bottom – the best way is to pour it through a funnel made from thin cardboard. Hold the bottle at a slight angle, while you do this so there is no danger of breaking it. Next add the potting compost, it too can be poured through the funnel. Should you wish to make your own compost use two parts of leaf-mould to each part of peat and gritty sand. Certain plants such as ferns and bromelias will also need some Sphagnum moss added to the mixture.

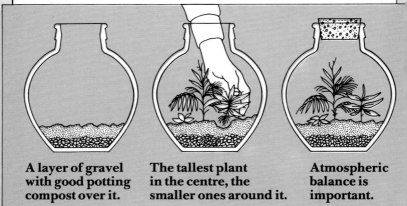

A layer of gravel with good potting compost over it.

The tallest plant in the centre, the smaller ones around it.

Atmospheric balance is important.

The planting process for the old acid jars requires a little inventiveness. Make small holes for your plants in the compost and then very carefully manoeuvre the plants into them pressing the earth down firmly around the roots. Some people use teaspoons attached to long sticks for this process. Dead leaves can be removed with a razor blade also attached to a long stick. Always remember to place the plants which will grow tallest in the middle of the bottle with the smaller plants around the edges.

The modern green jars are much simpler to use since they have wide necks which allow the work to be done by hand.

The atmosphere inside your bottle should not differ too much from that in your room. Leave the bottle open at the top until this atmosphere has developed properly – sometimes this can take several weeks. Condensation on the sides of the bottle indicates that the atmosphere has not yet properly developed. The top should only be placed on the bottle once the condensation has disappeared.

SUMMER AND WINTER

The natural growing cycle applies just as much to house plants as it does to those in your garden. Generally the Spring and Summer are the growing and flowering seasons while in the Autumn berries and other types of fruit ripen and in the Winter the plants rest. Therefore the plants need more light, humidity and warmth in the growing and flowering season. Once the Winter draws to a close and the resting period is over the plant must be prepared for the new growing and flowering season and this is the time for pruning, re-potting and freshening up your plants. Always bear in mind this cycle when caring for your plants.

With a little imagination, it is possible to think up a number of ways to provide your plants with enough water whilst you're away. You can buy one of the so-called plant-watchers available from specialized stores. They are made of water-absorbant foam. They work well in practice, because they help retain nutrients.

HOLIDAYS

What do you do with your plants when you go on holiday? It's a problem that many people encounter and it isn't sufficient to leave them and hope for the best.

Some are lucky enough to have neighbours with whom the plants can be left or who will come and tend to them during their absence. Many plants can cheerfully go out into the garden in the summer.

Dig them in, so that the rim of the pot is under the ground. This prevents the potting mixture from drying out. If you have to leave the plants in the house there are now a number of devices which make it possible to supply them with food and water over a period of several weeks. There is a sort of 'plant-sitter' made of water-absorbent foam which also contains nutrients.

The old-fashioned method is to place the plants around the bath supplying each plant with water by means of strands of wool which suck up and supply a slow but regular water ration. A similar system can be set up elsewhere with the aid of a large bucket or bowl. Always remember, however, not to leave them in bright sunlight or in an over-heated room while you are away.

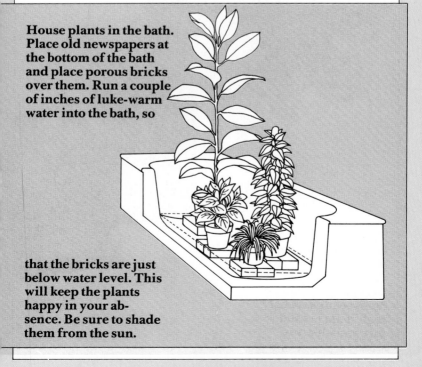

House plants in the bath. Place old newspapers at the bottom of the bath and place porous bricks over them. Run a couple of inches of luke-warm water into the bath, so

that the bricks are just below water level. This will keep the plants happy in your absence. Be sure to shade them from the sun.

EVERGREENS

The large group of evergreen plants enjoys ever-increasing popularity. This is hardly surprising since the great majority of them are relatively easy to care for. If they receive the regular attention which they require they can live happily for many years and provide a living decoration for both homes and offices.

Among the well-known varieties are *Calathea, Dieffenbachia, Ficus, Hypoestes, Philodendron, Tradescantia.*

The Asplenium is often used in arrangements, together with Calathea and Fittonia (right). All three varieties require a fairly high room temperature and plenty of water.

FERNS AND PALMS

Ferns and palms are varieties of evergreen which can give a great deal of pleasure over long periods and, as a result, have proved very popular. We deal with them separately here since they require a different type of care. In their natural state ferns grow in woods where the earth is relatively poor and usually occupy damp shady spots. Their character doesn't change when you bring them into your living room so give them the treatment which they need i.e. plenty of water and regular spraying. Do not stand them in the sun, give little or no plant food and do not keep them in an excessively warm room. Palms also need special treatment so look them up in the alphabetical list e.g. under *Chamaedorea, Cycas, Howeia* and *Phoenix*.

The palm in this picture is the Howeia (or Kentia) forsteriana, the fern is a Nephrolepsis or Boston Fern which likes shade.

FLOWERING PLANTS

Flowers make any room attractive but flowering house plants are even better since it is your care and attention which makes them bloom. If you are looking for the sense of satisfaction that comes from growing flowering house plants then consult the alphabetical list from pages 34-73. Your choice will naturally be influenced by colour, shape and the number of flowers which the plants produce as well as by the length of the flowering season. There are very many varieties which flower abundantly and among these are *Begonias, Geraniums, Saintpaulia* and *Azaleas*. None of these is expensive and if well tended can continue to give you pleasure over long periods. You will, however, come across some less well-known varieties in the alphabetical list – ones which will only flower after several years of intensive care. Before you buy these consider carefully whether you have the time and the inclination for such plants.

Saintpaulia, best-known as African Violet. Cross-breeding and selection have produced many different colours. These are inexpensive and highly rewarding house plants.

There are so many varieties of flowering house plants, that we only give one example here (for more, see pages 34-73).

The Azalea is a very old house plant, but still a superb plant for your living room.

The name literally means 'dry', but it would be a mistake to keep Azaleas dry for that reason. On the contrary, they require plenty of moisture whilst in flower. It is good to immerse this small shrub in luke-warm water once a week.

In Summer it is perfectly possible to keep the plant in the garden. Azaleas can't take direct sunlight, like many plants. Don't stand them over a radiator. Poor, acid soil is recommended, the soil has to be porous as well, for instance coarse-fibred peat-mould or woodland soil.

After flowering, stand the plant in a cool room, water it less, but don't let the root ball dry up.

CACTI AND SUCCULENT PLANTS

Although cacti were first imported into Europe from America in the seventeenth century it is only recently that they have started to become popular. The same cannot be said for succulent plants and there is still only a relatively small group of plant-lovers interested in such varieties.

The problems with both are largely due to the difficulties most people have with bringing them into flower. They grow rather slowly, change shape only gradually and as a result people often tire of them.

There are, however, many varieties of cacti which can easily be coaxed into flower e.g. *Rhipsalidopsis*. Succulent plants which can be brought into bloom include *Echeveria*.

ORCHIDS

Orchids are still regarded as rare and expensive and will always catch the eye in a vase where tulips or daisies might be overlooked. It is not widely known, however, that ten per cent of all our plants are orchids... there are several thousand varieties of them.

What is more, thanks to continuous improvements in growing techniques they are becoming increasingly available to the public. If you are interested in an orchid as a house plant, simply ask your supplier for a potted *Cattleya*, *Dendrobium* or *Odontoglossum*. There are various types of each, which are well-suited to your living-room.

BULBS AND TUBEROUS PLANTS

The words 'bulbs' and 'tubers' instantly bring to mind a garden full of flowering Crocuses, Snowdrops, Narcissi and Tulips. But we can all bring bulbs and tuberous plants into flower in the living room. For many years now, people have been growing Hyacinths in special glasses and this is probably the oldest form of hydroculture. However, Tulips, Crocuses, Narcissi and Hyacinths can also be grown in bulb fibre and the famous 'Paperwhite' Narcissi will grow happily in a bowl with gravel. Don't forget, either, the *Hippeastrum* (Amaryllis) which gives a taste of Spring during the Winter months.

HERBS

Why not grow your own herbs on a window sill? Try it with Chives: sow them at the beginning of April in a flower-pot filled with potting compost. Then why not put a pot of home-grown Parsley next to it and build up your stock of kitchen herbs with Garlic, Thyme, Rosemary, Marjoram, Sage, Lavender, Hysop, Mint... etc. It is not difficult and it is extremely rewarding.

ABUTILON hybride
Spotted flowering maple

Flowering season: Summer, Autumn, even in Winter. **Care:** When in bloom plenty of water. Light place, a little sunshine (morning sun), fresh air. Water sparingly after October. In Winter 10-12°C (50-55°F). **Feeding:** Once a fortnight during flowering season. **Propagation:** Cuttings under plastic. **Re-potting:** Every year, in Spring.

ACALYPHA hispida
Red hot cat's-tail

Flowering season: Spring-Autumn. **Care:** Plenty of luke-warm water when in bloom (island, page 80), spray regularly. Warm, light place, no direct sunlight. High air-humidity, 15-18°C (58-65°F). **Feeding:** Once a fortnight during Summer. **Propagation:** Cuttings under plastic, warm soil base. **Re-potting:** when necessary, in Spring.

ACALYPHA wilkesiana
Copper leaf

Flowering season: Spring-Autumn. **Care:** Plenty of luke-warm water (island), spray. Warm, light place, no direct sunlight. High air-humidity, 15-18°C. Keep plant short and bushy by nipping longest shoots from crown. **Propagation:** Cuttings under plastic, warm soil base. **Re-potting:** when necessary, Spring.

ACHIMENES 'Paul Arnold'
Cupid's bower

Flowering season: Spring-Autumn. **Care:** Plenty of luke-warm water when in bloom. Spray frequently. Warm, light place, no direct sunlight. High air-humidity. Keep dry over Winter. 13-16°C (55-60°F). **Feeding:** Once a fortnight only during flowering season. **Propagation:** Crown cuttings in peat or root division. **Re-potting:** Every year, in Spring.

ACHIMENES hybrids
Cupid's bower

Flowering season: Spring-Autumn. **Care:** Plenty of luke-warm water when in bloom. Spray frequently. Warm, light place, no direct sunlight. High air-humidity. Keep dry over Winter. 13-16°C (55-60°F). **Feeding:** Once a fortnight, only during flowering season. **Propagation:** Crown cutting in peat or roots division. **Re-potting:** Every year, in Spring.

ACORUS gramineus 'aureo-variegatus'
Sweet flag
Flowering season: None. **Care:** Plenty of water, rather dark place, keep covered during Winter. High air-humidity, 10-13°C (55-60°F). **Propagation:** Divide plants at any time. **Re-potting:** If necessary, in Spring.

ADIANTUM raddianum
(Acuneatum)
Maidenhair fern
Flowering season: None.
Care: Water regularly, spray
frequently. Light place, no
direct sunlight. Avoid
draughts. 15-20°C (60-70°
F). When the plant shrivels
up, cut it just above compost
in pot. **Feeding:** Not necessary. **Propagation:** Root
division, in Spring. **Re-
potting:** Every year, in
Spring.

AECHMEA fasciata
Urn plant

Flowering season: Spring-
Autumn. **Care:** Plenty of
luke-warm water on earth;
when not in bloom, also in
crown. Light place, no direct
sunlight. Loam: Anthurium
compound. 15-18°C.
Feeding: Once a week in
growing season. **Propagation:** Prune rosettes from 15
cm length and re-pot or
prune directly from mother-
plant after flowering season.

AECHMEA 'fascini'
Urn plant

Flowering season: Spring-
Autumn. **Care:** Plenty of
luke-warm water on earth;
when not in bloom, also in
crown. Light place, no direct
sunlight. Loam: Anthurium
compound. 15-18°C.
Feeding: Once a week in
growing season. **Propagation:** Prune rosettes from 15
cm length and re-pot or
prune directly from mother-
plant after flowering season.

AENONIUM arboreum

Flowering season: Spring.
Only the full-grown plants
produce golden-yellow
clusters. **Care:** Water
sparingly, give little or no
water during rest period.
Sunny place, low air-
humidity. Not below 10°C.
(50°F). Can go into the
garden in Summer. **Feeding:**
None. **Propagation:** Cuttings
or seed. **Re-potting:** April-
May when re-growing.

AESCHYNANTHUS radicans
Lipstick vine

Flowering season: Summer.
Care: Plenty of soft water on
compound, spray frequently.
Light place, but no sunlight.
High air-humidity, minimum
temperature 18°C (65°F).
Feeding: Once a fortnight.
Propagation: Stem cuttings
in February, under plastic.
Re-potting: If necessary, in
February.

AESCHYNANTHUS
obconicus
Lipstick vine
Flowering season: Summer.
Care: Plenty of water if
possible rain-water. Spray
frequently. Light place, but
no sunlight. High air-
humidity, preferably about
20°C (70°F). **Feeding:** Once
a fortnight. **Propagation:**
Head cuttings under plastic,
February. **Re-potting:** Not
strictly necessary, if wanted
in early Spring.

AGLAONEMA cummulatum
Chinese evergreen

Flowering season: Inconspicious, after that red currants. **Care:** Rather warm and damp place. Preferably constantly about 20°C (70° F). **Feeding:** In Spring and Summer, weekly. **Propagation:** Cuttings under plastic, in Spring. **Re-potting:** If necessary, in Spring.

ALOCASIA sanderiana
Bat wings

Flowering season: None. **Care:** Plenty of water in Summer, little water in Winter, warm place, no sun. High air-humidity, at least 16-22°C (60-70°F). Avoid draughts. **Feeding:** Occasionally, during Summer. **Propagation:** Root separation or seeding. **Re-potting:** If necessary, in Spring.

AMPELOPSIS variegata

Flowering season: None. **Care:** Plenty of water during growing season, little water during rest period. Light place, fresh air, no bright sunlight. Prune in Spring. Not below 10°C (50°F). **Feeding:** Once a fortnight during growing season. **Propagation:** Cuttings. **Re-potting:** If necessary, in Spring.

ANANAS comosus
(variegatus)
Pineapple plant
Flowering season: Seldom. **Care:** Medium amount of water, also in crown, spray frequently, keep roots moist, sunny place, high air-humidity, 16-22°C. **Feeding:** Once a month during growing season. **Propagation:** Ground shoots or green tuft cutting together with piece of fruit; plant under plastic in warm loam. **Re-potting:** In Spring.

ANTHURIUM
scherzerianum-hybr.
Flamingo flower
Flowering season: Spring-Autumn. **Care:** Plenty of luke-warm water, spray, sponge leaves regularly once a week. Light, warm place, no direct sunlight. High air-humidity. 15°C (58°F) minimum. Flowers suitable for floral arrangements. **Feeding:** Once a week when in bloom. **Propagation:** Root division. **Re-potting:** After flowering season.

APHELANDRA squarrosa
Zebra plant

Flowering season: Spring-Summer. **Care:** Light, warm place, no direct sunlight. Plenty of luke-warm, soft water when in bloom (island). Spray daily, sponge leaves regularly. Cut off dead heads and prune back stem. High air-humidity. 13°C (55° F) minimum. **Feeding:** Once a fortnight. **Propagation:** Head cuttings under plastic. **Re-potting:** After rest period.

ARALIA castor

Flowering season: None.
Care: This plant needs a
warm and damp place. Spray
each day with luke-warm
rain-water. Light place,
some sunlight permitted. At
least 16°C (60°F). **Feeding:**
Once a fortnight. **Propagation:** Difficult. **Re-potting:**
Each year in Spring.

ARALIA sieboldii
Castor oil plant

Flowering season: None.
Care: This plant needs a
warm and damp place. Spray
each day with luke-warm
rain-water. Light place,
some sunlight permitted.
Temperature at least 16°C
(60°F). **Feeding:** Once a
fortnight. **Propagation:**
Difficult. **Re-potting:** Each
year in Spring.

ARAUCARIA heterophylla
Norfolk Island pine

Flowering season: None.
Care: Plenty of luke-warm
water during Summer. Very
little water in Winter. Light,
cool place, no sunlight. Low
air-humidity, frost-free
temperature. **Feeding:** Once
a fortnight, in Summer only.
Propagation: Seedings,
possibly head cuttings. **Re-
potting:** Spring, in pine-
wood loam.

ARDISIA crenata
Coral berry

Flowering season: April-
May. **Care:** Plenty of water
on soil, spray leaves. Light,
not too warm place, a little
sunshine. Fairly high air-
humidity, 10-16°C
(50-60°F). **Feeding:** Once a
week when in flower.
Propagation: Seeding or
cuttings. **Re-potting:** Young
plants in Spring.

ASPARAGUS falcatus
Asparagus fern

Flowering season: Very
seldom, small white flowers.
Care: Plenty of water in
Summer, spray frequently.
Moderately light, warm
place, no direct sunlight,
avoid drying out of roots.
Fairly high air-humidity.
10-22°C (50-60°F). **Feeding:**
Once a fortnight, during
Summer. **Propagation:** Root
division in Spring, seeding.
Re-potting: Spring.

ASPARAGUS densiflorus
'Meyers'
Plume asparagus
Flowering season: None.
Care: Plenty of water during
Summer, spray frequently.
Temperate, light place, no
direct sunlight. Avoid drying
out of roots. Fairly high air-
humidity. 10-22°C. Has
more bushy branches than
'Sprengeri'. **Feeding:** Once a
fortnight in Summer.
Propagation: Root division
in Spring, seeding. **Re-
potting:** Every Spring.

ASPARAGUS setaceus
Asparagus fern

Flowering season: None.
Care: Plenty of water during
Summer, spray frequently.
Temperate, light place, no
direct sunlight. Avoid drying
out of roots. Fairly high air-
humidity. 10-22°C
(50-70°F). **Feeding:** Once a
fortnight during Summer.
Propagation: Root division
in Spring, seeding. **Re-
potting:** Every Spring.

ASPARAGUS densiflorus
'sprengeri'
Asparagus fern
Flowering season: None,
but sometimes produces
small, white flowers. **Care:**
Plenty of water in Summer,
spray frequently. Moderately
light, warm place, no direct
sunlight, avoid drying out of
roots. Fairly high air-
humidity. 10-22°C. **Feeding:**
Once a fortnight during
Summer. **Propagation:** Root
division in Spring, seeding.
Re-potting: Spring.

ASPLENIUM nidus
Bird's nest fern

Flowering season: None.
Care: Warm place, on dark
side. Plenty of soft water in
Summer (island). Spray
frequently, sponge leaves
once a week. High air-
humidity, 16-20°C
(60-70°F). **Feeding:** Once a
week. **Propagation:** Own
shoots. **Re-potting:** Spring,
every 2-3 years.

AZALIA indica
Indian azalea

Flowering season: Spring,
Autumn, Winter. **Care:**
Plenty of soft water when in
flower. Spray buds only,
luke-warm footbath once a
week. Light, cool place, no
sun. During rest period 10-
16°C, when in bloom max.
19°C. **Feeding:** regularly
during Summer. **Propaga-
tion:** Difficult. **Re-potting:**
Once every 2-3 years.

BEAUCARNEA recurnata
Ponytail plant

Flowering season: None.
Care: Reasonably light place,
no direct sun. Damp atmo-
sphere, spray frequently and
water (luke) on roots at least
twice a week. Equable temperature, in winter at least 10°C.
Feeding: Once a fortnight,
not in Winter. **Propagation:**
Difficult. **Re-potting:** Only
when pot becomes too
small, in Spring.

BEGONIA elatior-hybr.
Begonia

Flowering season:
Summer-Winter. **Care:**
Light place, no direct
sunlight. Luke-warm water
on soil when in bloom, keep
soil moist. Reasonably
warm, 16-22°C (60-70°F).
Remove dead heads.
Feeding: Once a week.
Propagation: Cuttings in
Spring. **Re-potting:**
Whenever necessary, do
not re-pot older plants.

BEGONIA 'Aphrodite'
Begonia

Flowering season: Summer-Winter. **Care:** Light place, no direct sunlight. Luke-warm water on soil when in bloom, keep soil moist. Reasonably warm, 16-22°C (60-70°F). Remove dead heads.
Feeding: Once a week.
Propagation: Cuttings in Spring. **Re-potting:** Whenever necessary; do not re-pot older plants.

BEGONIA Rex-hybr.
Rex Begonia

Flowering season: None.
Care: Luke-warm water on soil, no direct sunlight, reasonably light place. High air-humidity. 13-approx. 20° C (55-approx. 70°F).
Feeding: once a fortnight, March through September.
Propagation: Leaf cuttings with 4 cm stem. **Re-potting:** Spring.

BELOPERONE guttata
Shrimp plant

Flowering season: All-season. **Care:** Plenty of light, no direct sunshine but can go in the garden during Summer. Lots of water when in bloom, thereafter, little. Keep roots moist. Normal air-humidity, not below 10°C (50°F). **Feeding:** Once a fortnight when in bloom.
Propagation: Plant cuttings in warm soil. **Re-potting:** If necessary, in Spring.

PINUS parviflora
Dwarf tree

Flowering season: None.
Care: Indoors; moderate amount of water, spray daily with rainwater. Light place, no direct sunlight. Can spend a limited amount of time per year indoors. **Feeding:** Once a fortnight during Summer.
Propagation: Seeding, cuttings (difficult). **Re-potting:** Never. These little trees can grow very old and seldom grow above 80 cm.

BOUGAINVILLEA
Paper flower

Flowering season: Spring-Summer. **Care:** Warm, light place, no direct sunlight. Plenty of water when in bloom, spray crown. Water sparingly in Winter. Warm, but with fresh air. Keep in cool place (7-10°C) over Winter. High air-humidity. Prune back after flowering season. **Feeding:** Once a fortnight. **Propagation:** cuttings (a professional job).

BOUGAINVILLEA
spectabilis
'Dania'
Paper flower
Flowering season: Spring-Summer. **Care:** Warm, light place. Plenty of water when in bloom, spray crown. Water sparingly in Winter. Warm, but with fresh air. Keep in cool place (7-10°C) over Winter. High air-humidity. Prune back after flowering season. **Feeding:** Once a fortnight. **Propagation:** Cuttings.

BREYNIA disticha
'Roseopicta'

Flowering season: None.
Care: Water sparingly four
times a week, plenty of light,
no direct sun. Moderate air-
humidity. Temperature:
20-22°C (68-72°F). **Feeding:**
Once a fortnight. **Propagation:** Crown cuttings under
plastic, warm soil. **Re-
potting:** Every 2 years, in
Spring.

BROWALLIA
speciosa 'Major'
Bush violet
Flowering season: Depends
on seeding time. **Care:**
Plenty of light, no direct sun.
Water: medium-abundant.
Remove dead-heads. Normal
air-humidity. Temperature:
12-16°C (52-60°F). Can
spend the Summer in the
garden. **Feeding:** Once a
fortnight. **Propagation:**
Seeding or 1-year cuttings.
Re-potting: When necessary.

BRUNFELSIA calycina
**Yesterday, today and
tomorrow**
Flowering season: No
special period. **Care:** cool
place, no direct sunlight,
fresh air. Plenty of water
when in bloom. Spray daily,
but not on flowers. Air-
humidity: high. Tempera-
ture: moderate, in Winter 13-
15°C. **Feeding:** Once every 3
weeks whilst in bloom.
Propagation: Crown cuttings
under plastic. **Re-potting:**
Prune back after flowering.

DESERT CACTI, several types

Flowering season: Differing. **Care:** Light, warm
place. In Winter little or no
water, recommended
temperature 10°C. In Spring
gradually more water,
irregularly, when compost
is too dry. **Feeding:**
Moderately in Summer and
during flowering. **Propagation:** Seeding, cutting or
grafting, dependent on
species.

DESERT CACTI, grafted

Flowering season: None.
Care: Light, warm place.
Direct sun or high tempera-
tures in Summer do not
harm. In Winter little or no
water, recommended
temperature 10°C (50°F). In
Spring gradually more water,
irregularly, when compost is
too dry. **Feeding:** Moderately, in Summer. **Propagation:**
By grafting again. **Re-
potting:** Not recommended.

CALADIUM bicolor
Angel's wings

Flowering season: Sometimes in Spring. **Care:** Light,
warm place, no direct sun.
Plenty of water (island).
Spray frequently. High air-
humidity. Temperature: in
rest period 13°C, when
growing 17-20°C. **Feeding:**
Once a fortnight. **Propagation:** Root separation,
cuttings at beginning of
growing season. **Re-potting:**
In Spring.

CALATHEA (mixed)
Prayer plants

Flowering season: None.
Care: Moderate-lavish water, spray frequently. In Summer, light place but no direct sun. In Winter, cooler and dryer. High air-humidity. Temperature: 15-22°C (60-70°F). **Feeding:** Regularly during growing season. **Propagation:** Separation or shoot cuttings. **Re-potting:** Spring, pot should not be too big.

CALATHEA crocata

Flowering season: Differing.
Care: moderate-much water, spray frequently. In Summer, light place but no direct sun. In Winter, cooler and dryer. High air-humidity. Temperature: 15-22°C. **Feeding:** Regularly during growing season. **Propagation:** Separation or shoot cuttings. **Re-potting:** Spring, pot should not be too big.

CALATHEA lancifolia
Rattlesnake plant

Flowering season: None.
Care: Moderate-lavish water, spray frequently. In Summer, light place but no direct sun. In Winter, cooler and dryer. High air-humidity. Temperature: 15-22°C (60-70°F). **Feeding:** Regularly during growing season. **Propagation:** Separation or shoot cuttings. **Re-potting:** Spring, pot should not be too big.

CALATHEA lietzei

Flowering season: None.
Care: Moderate-lavish water, spray frequently. In Summer, light place but no direct sun. In Winter, cooler and dryer. High air-humidity. Temperature: 15-22°C (60-70°F). **Feeding:** Regularly during growing season. **Propagation:** Separation or shoot cuttings. **Re-potting:** Spring, pot should not be too big.

CALATHEA louisae

Flowering season: None.
Care: Moderate-lavish water, spray frequently. In Summer, light place but no direct sun. In Winter, cooler and dryer. High air-humidity. Temperature: 15-22°C (60-70°F). **Feeding:** Regularly during growing season. **Propagation:** Separation or shoot cuttings. **Re-potting:** Spring, pot should not be too big.

CALATHEA makoyana
Peacock plant

Flowering season: None.
Care: Moderate-lavish water, spray frequently. In Summer, light place but no direct sun. In Winter, cooler and dryer. High air-humidity. Temperature: 15-22°C (60-70°F). **Feeding:** Regularly during growing season. **Propagation:** Separation or shoot cuttings. **Re-potting:** Spring, pot should not be too big.

CALATHEA ornata
'Sanderiana'

Flowering season: None.
Care: Moderate-lavish water, spray frequently. In Summer, light place but no direct sun. In Winter, cooler and dryer. High air-humidity. Temperature: 15-22°C (60-70°F). **Feeding:** Regularly during growing season. **Propagation:** Separation or shoot cuttings. **Re-potting:** Spring, pot should not be too big.

CALATHEA picturata
'Argentea'

Flowering season: None.
Care: Moderate-lavish water, spray frequently. In Summer, light place but no direct sun. In Winter, cooler and dryer. High air-humidity. Temperature: 15-22°C (60-70°F). **Feeding:** Regularly during growing season. **Propagation:** Separation or shoot cuttings. **Re-potting:** Spring, pot should not be too big.

CALATHEA roseo-picta

Flowering season: None.
Care: Moderate-lavish water, spray frequently. In Summer, light place but no direct sun. In Winter, cooler and dryer. High air-humidity. Temperature: 15-22°C (60-70°F). **Feeding:** Regularly during growing season. **Propagation:** Separation or shoot cuttings. **Re-potting:** Spring, pot should not be too big.

CALATHEA zebrina
Zebra plant

Flowering season: None.
Care: Moderate-lavish water, spray frequently. In Summer, light place but no direct sun. In Winter, cooler and dryer. High air-humidity. Temperature: 15-22°C (60-70°F). **Feeding:** Regularly during growing season. **Propagation:** Separation or shoot cuttings. **Re-potting:** Spring, pot should not be too big.

CALCEOLARIA
herbeohybrida
Slipper flower
Flowering season: May-June. **Care:** Moderate amount of water on soil, spray frequently. Light, cool place, no direct sun. Normal air-humidity. Temperature: 15-20°C (60-70°F). **Feeding:** Once a fortnight. **Propagation:** Seeding (difficult). **Re-potting:** Never necessary (annual).

CAMPANULA isophylla
Italian bell flower

Flowering season: Summer and Autumn. **Care:** Keep soil moist, light, cool place, no direct sun. Remove deadheads daily. Prune back flower stems after blooming. Can spend Summer in the garden. Medium air-humidity. Winter temperature: 6-8°C. **Feeding:** Once a fortnight in Summer. **Propagation:** Cuttings. **Re-potting:** in Spring.

CANNA Indica-hybr.

Flowering season: Summer-Autumn. **Care:** Plenty of water during growing season. Light place, no direct sun. Does better in the garden during Summer. Medium air-humidity. Winter temperature: 15°C (60°F). **Feeding:** Once a week. **Propagation:** Seeding or stalk cuttings with node. **Re-potting:** Early Spring.

CAPSICUM annuum
Pepper plant

Flowering season: Summer; red currants in Autumn and Winter. **Care:** Light and airy place, by preference sun. Room temperature: compost not too damp (to avoid mould). Watch out for lice. **Feeding:** At most once every three weeks. **Propagation:** Seeding, March-April.

CEREUS monstrosus

Flowering season: Only flowers out-of-doors. **Care:** Plenty of water in Summer, little in Winter. Light, sunny place, low air-humidity, high temperature, not below 10°C (50°F). **Feeding:** None. **Propagation:** Seeding, cuttings. **Re-potting:** in Spring, when necessary.

CEROPEGIA debilis woodii
Rosary vine

Flowering season: Summer. **Care:** Not too much water, dry, sunny place, low air-humidity. Temperature: Summer 15-22, Winter 10-15°C (50-60°F). **Feeding:** Once a fortnight during growing season. **Propagation:** Cuttings: stem and/or axil-sections. **Re-potting:** Seldom. When necessary, in Spring.

CHAMAEDOREA elegans
Parlour palm

Flowering season: Winter (sporadic). **Care:** Plenty of water on soil, spray frequently. Light, but not sunny place. High air-humidity. Temperature: 12-20°C, (55-70°F). **Feeding:** Once every three weeks during Summer. **Propagation:** Seeding. **Re-potting:** Spring, when necessary.

CHAMAEDOREA elegans
Parlour palm

Flowering season: Winter (sporadic). **Care:** Plenty of water on soil, spray frequently. Light, but not sunny place. High air-humidity. Temperature: 12-20°C (55-70°F). **Feeding:** Once every three weeks during Summer. **Propagation:** Seeding. **Re-potting:** Spring, when necessary.

CHLOROPHYTUM capense
'Mediopictum'
Spider plant
Flowering season: Spring-
Summer. **Care:** Water daily
in Summer, give less water
in Winter. Spray frequently.
Light, warm, not too dry
place, no direct sunlight. Air-
humidity: not too low.
Temperature: Summer 18-
22°C, Winter 10-12°C.
Feeding: Once a week in
Summer, in Winter none.
Propagation: Separate and
pot offsprings.

CHRYSALIDOCARPUS
lutescens
Areca palm
Flowering season: None.
Care: Fairly high temperature, about 25°C (75°F), at
night at least 15°C (60°F).
Damp atmosphere, place jar
in a bowl permanently filled
with water. No direct sun.
Feeding: Once a fortnight.
Propagation: Seeding. **Re-
potting:** Not necessary.

CISSUS antarctica
Kangaroo vine

Flowering season: None.
Care: Medium quantity of
luke-warm water on soil,
spray in Winter. Light place,
no direct sunlight. Air-
humidity: normal. Temperature: medium to cool.
Feeding: Once a month, but
not during rest period.
Propagation: Cuttings from
top or stem sections. **Re-
potting:** Young plants, in
Spring.

CISSUS 'Leea Coccinea'

Flowering season: None.
Care: Medium quantity of
luke-warm water on soil,
spray in Winter. Light place,
no direct sunlight. Air-
humidity: normal. Temperature: medium to cool.
Feeding: Once a month, but
not during rest period.
Propagation: Cuttings from
top or stem sections. **Re-
potting:** Young plants, in
Spring.

CITROFORTUNELLA mitis
Orange tree

Flowering season: May,
bears fruit thereafter. **Care:**
Plenty of soft water during
growing and flowering
season, Winter little. Spray
when not in flower. Air-
humidity: not too low.
Temperature: in Winter 5-8°
C. **Feeding:** Once a week
during growing and flowering season. **Propagation:**
Cuttings (difficult). **Re-
potting:** Spring.

CLERODENDRON
thomsanae
Glory bower
Flowering season: May.
Care: water daily, giving less
water in Winter. Spray
frequently. Light place, no
direct sunlight, prune in early
Spring. Normal air-humidity.
Temperature 10-15°C.
Feeding: Only during
growing and flowering
season. **Propagation:** Root
and shoot cuttings. **Re-
potting:** Shortly before start
of growing season.

CLERODENDRON splendens

Flowering season: May.
Care: Water daily, giving less water in Winter. Spray frequently. Light place, no direct sunlight, prune in early Spring. Normal air-humidity. Temperature: 10-15°C.
Feeding: Only during growing and flowering season. **Propagation:** Root and shoot cuttings. **Re-potting:** Shortly before start of growing season.

CLIVIA minitia-hybr.
Kaffir lily

Flowering season: February-March. **Care:** Plenty of water when in flower, little in Winter. Sponge leaves regularly. Permanent, cool place, no direct sunlight. Normal air-humidity. Winter temperature 10°C. **Feeding:** Once a week from April through August. **Propagation:** Offsprings (side shoots). **Re-potting:** After flowering, if necessary.

COCOS nucifera
Coconut palm

Flowering season: None.
Care: Water regularly, spray, give a luke-warm bath once in a while. Keep roots moist. Very light, warm place. Do not plant in a tall pot. High air-humidity. High temperature: 20-23°C (68-72°F). The durability of this plant is limited. **Feeding:** Once a week in Summer. **Propagation:** Seeding (hot bed). **Re-potting:** Never.

CODIAEUM variegatum-hybr.
Joseph's coat
Flowering season: None.
Care: Luke-warm water, according to environment, on soil. Spray often, sponge leaves regularly. Light, sunny place, high air-humidity. Temperature: 18-22°C. **Feeding:** Once a fortnight over the Summer. **Propagation:** Cuttings (difficult). **Re-potting:** In Spring, if necessary.

CODIAEUM 'Aucubaefolium'

Flowering season: None.
Care: Luke-warm water, according to environment, on soil. Spray often, sponge leaves regularly. Light, sunny place, high air-humidity. Temperature: 18-22°C (64-70°F). **Feeding:** Once a fortnight over the Summer. **Propagation:** Cuttings (difficult). **Re-potting:** In Spring, if necessary.

CODIAEUM 'Bravo'

Flowering season: None.
Care: Luke-warm water, according to environment, on soil. Spray often, sponge leaves regularly. Light, sunny place, high air-humidity. Temperature: 18-22°C (64-70°F). **Feeding:** Once a fortnight over the Summer. **Propagation:** Cuttings (difficult). **Re-potting:** In Spring, if necessary.

CODIAEUM 'Excellent'

Flowering season: None.
Care: Luke-warm water, according to environment, on soil. Spray often, sponge leaves regularly. Light, sunny place, high air-humidity. Temperature: 18-22°C (64-70°F). **Feeding:** Once a fortnight over the Summer. **Propagation:** Cuttings (difficult). **Re-potting:** In Spring, if necessary.

CODIAEUM 'Gold Star'

Flowering season: None.
Care: Luke-warm water, according to environment, on soil. Spray often, sponge leaves regularly. Light, sunny place, high air-humidity. Temperature: 18-22°C (64-70°F). **Feeding:** Once a fortnight over the Summer. **Propagation:** Cuttings (difficult). **Re-potting:** In Spring, if necessary.

CODIAEUM 'Iceton'

Flowering season: None.
Care: Luke-warm water, according to environment, on soil. Spray often, sponge leaves regularly. Light, sunny place, high air-humidity. Temperature: 18-22°C (64-70°F). **Feeding:** Once a fortnight over the Summer. **Propagation:** Cuttings (difficult). **Re-potting:** In Spring, if necessary.

CODIAEUM 'Nervia'

Flowering season: None.
Care: Luke-warm water, according to environment, on soil. Spray often, sponge leaves regularly. Light, sunny place, high air-humidity. Temperature: 18-22°C (64-70°F). **Feeding:** Once a fortnight over the Summer. **Propagation:** Cuttings (difficult). **Re-potting:** In Spring, if necessary.

CODIAEUM 'Norma'

Flowering season: None.
Care: Luke-warm water, according to environment, on soil. Spray often, sponge leaves regularly. Light, sunny place, high air-humidity. Temperature: 18-22°C (64-70°F). **Feeding:** Once a fortnight over the Summer. **Propagation:** Cuttings (difficult). **Re-potting:** In Spring, if necessary.

CODIAEUM 'Philippe Geduldig'

Flowering season: None.
Care: Luke-warm water, according to environment, on soil. Spray often, sponge leaves regularly. Light, sunny place, high air-humidity. Temperature: 18-22°C. **Feeding:** Once a fortnight over the Summer. **Propagation:** Cuttings (difficult). **Re-potting:** In Spring, if necessary.

CODIAEUM 'Sunny star'

Flowering season: None.
Care: Luke-warm water,
according to environment,
on soil. Spray often, sponge
leaves regularly. Light,
sunny place, high air-
humidity. Temperature:
18-22°C (64-70°F). **Feeding:**
Once a fortnight over the
Summer. **Propagation:**
Cuttings (difficult). **Re-
potting:** In Spring, if necessary.

COLEUS Blumei-hybr.
Flame nettle

Flowering season: None.
Care: Water copiously every
day during Summer. In
Winter give less water. Light,
airy, sunny place. High air-
humidity. Temperature:
18-22°C (64-70°F). **Feeding:**
Once a fortnight over the
Summer. **Propagation:**
Cuttings (difficult). **Re-
potting:** When necessary.

COLUMNEA microphylla
Goldfish plant

Flowering season: Nov.-
Apr. **Care:** Plenty of luke-
warm water during growth
and flowering season, water
less in Winter. Spray until
flower-buds take on colour.
Light place, no direct
sunlight. High air-humidity.
Temperature: 16-22°C.
Feeding: Once a week during
growing season. **Propagation:** Cuttings. **Re-potting:** If
necessary: April-May.

CORDYLINE-hybr.

Flowering season: Sporadic. **Care:** Do not over-water,
spray daily, sponge leaves
regularly. Light place, no
direct sunlight. High air-
humidity. Temperature:
17-22°C (62-70°F). **Feeding:**
Once a fortnight during
Summer. **Propagation:**
Cuttings. **Re-potting:** Young
plants: yearly, later once
every 2-3 years.

CORDYLINE 'Atom'

Flowering season: Sporadic, only old plants. **Care:** Do
not over-water, spray daily,
sponge leaves regularly.
Light place, no direct
sunlight. High air-humidity.
Temperature: 17-22°C
(62-70°F). **Feeding:** Once a
fortnight during Summer.
Propagation: Cuttings. **Re-
potting:** Young plants:
yearly, later once every 2-3
years.

CORDYLINE 'Kiwi'

Flowering season: Sporadic, only old plants. **Care:** Do
not over-water, spray daily,
sponge leaves regularly.
Light place, no direct
sunlight. High air-humidity.
Temperature: 17-22°C
(62-70°F). **Feeding:** Once a
fortnight during Summer.
Propagation: Cuttings. **Re-
potting:** Young plants:
yearly, later once every 2-3
years.

CORDYLINE 'Lord Robinson'

Flowering season: Sporadic, only old plants. **Care:** Do not over-water, spray daily, sponge leaves regularly. Light place, no direct sunlight. High air-humidity. Temperature: 17-22°C (62-70°F). **Feeding:** Once a fortnight during Summer. **Propagation:** Cuttings. **Repotting:** Young plants: yearly, later once every 2-3 years.

CORDYLINE terminus
Red edge

Flowering season: Sporadic, only old plants. **Care:** Do not over-water, spray daily, sponge leaves regularly. Light place, no direct sunlight. High air-humidity. Temperature: 17-22°C (62-70°F). **Feeding:** Once a fortnight during Summer. **Propagation:** Cuttings. **Repotting:** Young plants: yearly, later once every 2-3 years.

CRASSULA argentea
Jade plant

Flowering season: Varying, dependent on grower; fairly long-lasting. **Care:** Very light and sunny place, close to the window (all seasons). Compost has to drain well. Do not over-water. Temperature in Winter can be cool, preferably about 10°C (50°F). **Feeding:** Sparingly during flowering-season. **Propagation:** Difficult, not recommended.

CROSSANDRA
infundibuli formis
Firecracker flower
Flowering season: Spring-Autumn. **Care:** In Summer plenty of water, little in Winter. Spray with lukewarm water. Moderately light place, no direct sunlight. Prune back after flowering. High air-humidity. Temperature: 12-18°C. **Feeding:** Once a fortnight during flowering season. **Propagation:** Cuttings. **Re-potting:** Spring.

CTENANTHE oppenheimiana
Never never plant

Flowering season: None. **Care:** Moderate amount of water, spray in Spring and Summer. Fairly light place, no sun. High air-humidity. Temperature: 18-22°C (64-70°F). **Feeding:** In Summer only, once a fortnight. **Propagation:** Root separation or shoot cuttings. **Re-potting:** Once every two years, in Spring.

CYCAS revoluta
Sago palm

Flowering season: None. **Care:** Moderate amount of water during growing season, thereafter little. Sponge leaves occasionally. Light place, cool and dry in Winter at a temperature of around 5°C (40°F). **Feeding:** Regularly during growing season. **Propagation:** Seeding (difficult). **Re-potting:** Every 2-3 years.

CYCLAMEN Persicum

Flowering season: Autumn-Spring. **Care:** Soft, luke-warm water round edge of pot or in saucer. Pour off surplus water. Moderate air-humidity. Average temperature: 10-15°C (50-60°F). **Feeding:** Once a week when in flower. **Propagation:** Seeding (difficult). **Re-potting:** Beginning of May.

**CYMBIDIUM
Orchid**

Flowering season: November-May. **Care:** Keep well moist all the year round. Light place, fresh air. Does best out-of-doors (in shade). Fairly high air-humidity. Temperature in Winter 10-20°C, in Summer max. 30°C. **Feeding:** Once a fortnight during Summer. **Propagation:** Cuttings or seeding (difficult). **Re-potting:** After flowering.

**CYPERUS alternifolius
Umbrella plant**

Flowering season: Spring-Summer. **Care:** Plenty of water, keep roots under water. Spray regularly. Light place, no sun. High air-humidity. Temperature reasonably cool. **Feeding:** Once a fortnight during growing and flowering season. **Propagation:** Root separation and/or cuttings. **Re-potting:** Only when necessary.

**DAVALLIA bullata
Rabbitsfoot fern**

Flowering season: None. **Care:** Davallia needs a tropical atmosphere: damp and warm. Even in Winter temperature not beneath 18°C. Place the pot in a bowl, filled with luke-warm water and spray daily. **Feeding:** Not necessary. **Propagation:** By cutting pieces of the root-stock; put them on damp sphagnum, under plastic. **Re-potting:** Spring.

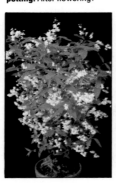

DEUTZIA gracilis

Flowering season: May-June. **Care:** Light place, no direct sunlight. Temperature 10-20°C, keep cool in Winter, 5-10°C. Spray regularly, give plenty of (soft) water in late Spring and Summer. **Feeding:** In flowering season and Summer once a fortnight. **Propagation:** Shoot cuttings, June-July. **Re-potting:** Before flowering.

**DIEFFENBACHIA amoena
Leopard lily**

Flowering season: Spring. **Care:** Plenty of soft, luke-warm water (island). Spray daily, also in Winter. Reasonably light place, no sun. Very high air-humidity. Temperature: Winter 18-20°C (64-68°F). **Feeding:** Once a fortnight during growing season. **Propagation:** Top cuttings or air layering. **Re-potting:** Spring.

DIEFFENBACHIA 'Camilla'

Flowering season: Spring.
Care: Plenty of soft, luke-warm water (island). Spray daily, also in Winter. Reasonably light place, no sun. Very high air-humidity. Temperature: Winter 18-20°C (64-68°F). **Feeding:** Once a fortnight during growing season. **Propagation:** Top cuttings or air layering. **Re-potting:** Spring.

DIEFFENBACHIA 'Marianne'

Flowering season: Spring.
Care: Plenty of soft, luke-warm water (island). Spray daily, also in Winter. Reasonably light place, no sun. Very high air-humidity. Temperature: Winter 18-20°C (64-68°F). **Feeding:** Once a fortnight during growing season. **Propagation:** Top cuttings or air layering. **Re-potting:** Spring.

DIEFFENBACHIA 'Tropic snow'

Flowering season: Spring.
Care: Plenty of soft, luke-warm water (island). Spray daily, also in Winter. Reasonably light place, no sun. Very high air-humidity. Temperature: Winter 18-20°C (64-68°F). **Feeding:** Once a fortnight during growing season. **Propagation:** Top cuttings or air layering. **Re-potting:** Spring.

DIEFFENBACHIA 'Veerle'

Flowering season: Spring.
Care: Plenty of soft, luke-warm water (island). Spray daily, also in Winter. Reasonably light place, no sun. Very high air-humidity. Temperature: Winter 18-20°C (64-68°F). **Feeding:** Once a fortnight during growing season. **Propagation:** Top cuttings or air layering. **Re-potting:** Spring.

DIZYGOTHECA elegantissima
Finger aralia
Flowering season: None.
Care: Moderate amount of soft water (island). Spray regularly, keep roots well moist. Light place, no sun, avoid draughts. Very high air-humidity. Temperature: 16-22°C. **Feeding:** Once a fortnight during growing season. **Propagation:** Seeding, cuttings (difficult). **Re-potting:** Spring, in coniferous loam.

DRACAENA fragrans
Corn plant

Flowering season: Spring and Summer. **Care:** Plenty of water (island), spray regularly, sponge leaves. Light, warm place, no sun, avoid draughts. High air-humidity. Temperature: 16-22°C (60-70°F). **Feeding:** Once a fortnight from March through October. **Propagation:** Seeding, head cuttings, stem-sections. **Re-potting:** In Spring, if necessary.

DRACAENA fragrans
'Massangeana'

Flowering season: Spring
and Summer. **Care:** Plenty of
water (island), spray
regularly, sponge leaves.
Light, warm place, no sun.
Avoid draughts. High air-
humidity. Temperature:
16-22°C (60-70°F). **Feeding:**
Once a fortnight from March
through October. **Propagation:** Seeding, head cuttings,
stem-sections. **Re-potting:**
In Spring, if necessary.

DRACAENA godseffiana
Florida beauty

Flowering season: Spring
and Summer. **Care:** Plenty of
water (island), spray
regularly, sponge leaves.
Light, warm place, no sun.
Avoid draughts. High air-
humidity. Temperature:
16-22°C (60-70°F). **Feeding:**
Once a fortnight from March
through October. **Propagation:** Seeding, head cuttings,
stem-sections. **Re-potting:**
In Spring, if necessary.

DRACAENA fragrans
'Massangeana'

Flowering season: Spring
and Summer. **Care:** Plenty of
water (island), spray
regularly, sponge leaves.
Light, warm place, no sun.
Avoid draughts. High air-
humidity. Temperature:
16-22°C (60-70°F). **Feeding:**
Once a fortnight from March
through October. **Propagation:** Seeding, head cuttings,
stem-sections. **Re-potting:**
In Spring, if necessary.

DRACAENA marginata
Dragon tree

Flowering season: Spring
and Summer. **Care:** Plenty of
water (island), spray
regularly, sponge leaves.
Light, warm place, no sun.
Avoid draughts. High air-
humidity. Temperature:
16-22°C (60-70°F). **Feeding:**
Once a fortnight from March
through October. **Propagation:** Seeding, head cuttings,
stem-sections. **Re-potting:**
In Spring, if necessary.

DRACAENA marginata
'Colorama'

Flowering season: Spring
and Summer. **Care:** Plenty of
water (island), spray
regularly, sponge leaves.
Light, warm place, no sun.
Avoid draughts. High air-
humidity. Temperature:
16-22°C (60-70°F). **Feeding:**
Once a fortnight from March
through October. **Propagation:** Seeding, head cuttings,
stem-sections. **Re-potting:**
In Spring, if necessary.

DRACAENA marginata
'Tricolor'

Flowering season: Spring
and Summer. **Care:** Plenty of
water (island), spray
regularly, sponge leaves.
Light, warm place, no sun.
Avoid draughts. High air-
humidity. Temperature:
16-22°C (60-70°F). **Feeding:**
Once a fortnight from March
through October. **Propagation:** Seeding, head cuttings,
stem-sections. **Re-potting:**
In Spring, if necessary.

DRACAENA sanderiana
Ribbon plant

Flowering season: Spring
and Summer. **Care:** Plenty of
water (island), spray
regularly, sponge leaves.
Light, warm place, no sun.
Avoid draughts. High air-
humidity. Temperature:
16-22°C (60-70°F). **Feeding:**
Once a fortnight from March
through October. **Propagation:** Seeding, head cuttings,
stem-sections. **Re-potting:**
In Spring, if necessary.

DRACAENA deremensis
'Warneckei'

Flowering season: Spring
and Summer. **Care:** Plenty of
water (island), spray
regularly, sponge leaves.
Light, warm place, no sun.
Avoid draughts. High air-
humidity. Temperature:
16-22°C (60-70°F). **Feeding:**
Once a fortnight from March
through October. **Propagation:** Seeding, head cuttings,
stem-sections. **Re-potting:**
In Spring, if necessary.

ECHEVERIA-hybr.

Flowering season: Depend-
ing upon variety. **Care:**
Summer normal, Winter little
or no water. Can stand out-
of-doors during the Sum-
mer. Light, airy and sunny
place. Winter temperature:
6-10°C (40-50°F). **Feeding:**
None. **Propagation:** Leaf
cuttings (rosette). **Re-
potting:** After plant has
finished flowering.

EPIPHYLLUM (hybrid)
Orchid cactus

Flowering season: Spring-
Summer. **Care:** Plenty of
water once plant after
flowering. Spray. Whilst
buds are forming, do not
turn the plant around. Light,
warm place, no direct sun.
Can go outside when no
longer blooming. High air-
humidity when growing.
Winter temperature 8-12°C.
Feeding: Once a fortnight
during Summer.

ERICA gracilis

Flowering season: Depend-
ing on variety. **Care:** Rainwater daily. Spray. Light, cool
place, a little sun. Air-
humidity: not too low.
Temperature: Summer max.
15, Winter min. 5°C (resp.
60 and 40°F). Does best out-
of-doors. **Feeding:** None.
Propagation: Cuttings. **Re-
potting:** None (difficult to
keep for long in-doors).

EUONYMUS-hybr.

Flowering season: None.
Care: Not too much water,
spray regularly. Light, cool
place. Normal air-humidity.
Temperature: Summer 10-
15, Winter 5-10°C. **Feeding:**
Once a fortnight from Spring
through Autumn. **Propagation:** Cuttings under plastic.
Re-potting: Early Spring.

EUPHORBIA lohmii

Flowering season: Regular.
Care: Plenty of water during growing/flowering season, little during resting period. Light, sunny place with plenty of fresh air. Fairly low air-humidity. Temperature: 15-20°C. **Feeding:** Once a fortnight during growing season. **Propagation:** Cuttings, treat wound with cigar-ash. **Re-potting:** After end of flowering season.

EUPHORBIA milii
Crown of thorns

Flowering season: Regular.
Care: Plenty of water during growing/flowering season, little during resting period. Light, sunny place with plenty of fresh air. Fairly low air-humidity. Temperature: 15-20°C. **Feeding:** Once a fortnight during growing season. **Propagation:** Cuttings, treat wound with cigar-ash. **Re-potting:** After end of flowering season.

EUPHORBIA (Poinsettia) pulcherrima
Poinsettia
Flowering season: Regular.
Care: Plenty of water during growing/flowering season, little during resting period. Light, sunny place with plenty of fresh air. Fairly low air-humidity. Temperature: 15-20°C. **Feeding:** Once a fortnight during growing season. **Propagation:** Cuttings, treat wound with cigar-ash. **Re-potting:** After end of flowering season.

EUPHORBIA triangularis

Flowering season: None.
Care: Plenty of water in Summer, little in Winter. Light, sunny place, fresh air. Relatively low air-humidity. Temperature 15-20°C (60-68°F). **Feeding:** Once a fortnight during growing season. **Propagation:** Cuttings. **Re-potting:** Just before start of growing season.

FATSHEDERA lizei
Ivy tree

Flowering season: None.
Care: Plenty of water during growing season, less thereafter. Sponge leaves once a week. Light place, fresh air, no sun. Air-humidity: not too low. Temperature: Summer 18°C, Winter 10-12°C. **Feeding:** Once a fortnight during growing season. **Propagation:** 15 cm head-cuttings in September, under plastic.

FATSHEDERA lizei 'Annemieke'

Flowering season: None.
Care: Plenty of water during growing season. Light place, fresh air, no sun. Spray occasionally. Air-humidity: not too low. Temperature: Summer 18°C, Winter 10-12°C. **Feeding:** Once a fortnight during growing season. **Propagation:** Cuttings in September, under plastic (air layering).

FATSHEDERA lizei 'Silver Prusca'

Flowering season: None.
Care: Plenty of water during growing season, less thereafter. Sponge leaves once a week. Light place, fresh air. Air-humidity: not too low. Temperature: Summer 18°C, Winter 10-12°C. **Feeding:** Once a fortnight during growing season. **Propagation:** Cuttings in September, under plastic.

FATSIA japonica
Castor oil plant

Flowering season: None.
Care: Plenty of water in Summer, little in Winter. Light cool place, no sun. Can stand outside during summer, in shade. Air-humidity: not too low. Temperature: cool, in Winter 4-10°C. **Feeding:** Once a fortnight during Summer. **Propagation:** Head or stem cuttings. **Re-potting:** In Spring, if necessary.

FICUS elastica 'Abidjan'

Flowering season: None.
Care: In Summer, plenty of luke-warm water. During rest-period (Oct.-Feb.) give less water. Warm, not too light place, no direct sunlight. Sponge leaves regularly. Do not turn plant around. Temperature: 15-22°C.
Feeding: Once a fortnight, exclusively during growing season. **Propagation:** Air and/or ground layering.

FICUS benjamina
Weeping fig

Flowering season: None.
Care: In Summer, plenty of luke-warm water. During rest-period (Oct.-Feb.) give less water. Warm, not too light place, no direct sunlight. Sponge leaves regularly. Do not turn plant around. Temperature: 15-22°C.
Feeding: Once a fortnight, exclusively during growing season. **Propagation:** Air and/or ground layering.

FICUS deltoidea (diversifolia)

Flowering season: None.
Care: In Summer, plenty of luke-warm water. During rest-period (Oct.-Feb.) give less water. Warm, not too light place, no direct sunlight. Sponge leaves regularly. Do not turn plant around. Temperature: 15-22°C.
Feeding: Once a fortnight, exclusively during growing season. **Propagation:** Air and/or ground layering.

FICUS elastica 'Schryveriana'

Flowering season: None.
Care: In Summer, plenty of luke-warm water. During rest-period (Oct.-Feb.) give less water. Warm, not too light place, no direct sunlight. Sponge leaves regularly. Do not turn plant around. Temperature: 15-22°C.
Feeding: Once a fortnight, exclusively during growing season. **Propagation:** Air and/or ground layering.

FICUS elastica 'Decora'

Flowering season: None.
Care: In Summer, plenty of luke-warm water. During rest-period (Oct.-Feb.) give less water. Warm, not too light place, no direct sunlight. Sponge leaves regularly. Do not turn plant around. Temperature: 15-22°C.
Feeding: Once a fortnight, exclusively during growing season. **Propagation:** Air and/or ground layering.

FICUS elastica 'Robusta'
Rubber plant

Flowering season: None.
Care: In Summer, plenty of luke-warm water. During rest-period (Oct.-Feb.) give less water. Warm, not too light place, no direct sunlight. Sponge leaves regularly. Do not turn plant around. Temperature: 15-22°C.
Feeding: Once a fortnight, exclusively during growing season. **Propagation:** Air and/or ground layering.

FICUS retusa 'Hawaii'

Flowering season: None.
Care: In Summer, plenty of luke-warm water. During rest-period (Oct.-Feb.) give less water. Warm, not too light place, no direct sunlight. Sponge leaves regularly. Do not turn plant around. Temperature: 15-22°C.
Feeding: Once a fortnight, exclusively during growing season. **Propagation:** Air and/or ground layering.

FICUS lyrata

Flowering season: None.
Care: In Summer, plenty of luke-warm water. During rest-period (Oct.-Feb.) give less water. Warm, not too light place, no direct sunlight. Sponge leaves regularly. Do not turn plant around. Temperature: 15-22°C.
Feeding: Once a fortnight, exclusively during growing season. **Propagation:** Air and/or ground layering.

FICUS Americana

Flowering season: None.
Care: In Summer, plenty of luke-warm water. During rest-period (Oct.-Feb.) give less water. Warm, not too light place, no direct sunlight. Sponge leaves regularly. Do not turn plant around. Temperature: 15-22°C.
Feeding: Once a fortnight, exclusively during growing season. **Propagation:** Air and/or ground layering.

FICUS pumila
Creeping fig

Flowering season: None.
Care: In Summer, plenty of luke-warm water. During rest-period (Oct.-Feb.) give less water. Warm, not too light place, no direct sunlight. Sponge leaves regularly. Do not turn plant around. Temperature: 15-22°C.
Feeding: Once a fortnight, exclusively during growing season. **Propagation:** Air and/or ground layering.

FICUS stricta

Flowering season: None.
Care: In Summer, plenty of luke-warm water. During rest-period (Oct.-Feb.) give less water. Warm, not too light place, no direct sunlight. Sponge leaves regularly. Do not turn plant around. Temperature: 15-22°C.
Feeding: Once a fortnight, exclusively during growing season. **Propagation:** Air and/or ground layering.

FICUS 'Westland'

Flowering season: None.
Care: In Summer, plenty of luke-warm water. During rest-period (Oct.-Feb.) give less water. Warm, not too light place, no direct sunlight. Sponge leaves regularly. Do not turn plant around. Temperature: 15-22°C.
Feeding: Once a fortnight, exclusively during growing season. **Propagation:** Air and/or ground layering.

FITTONIA verschaffeltii
Nerve plant

Flowering season: None.
Care: Plenty of water in Summer, less in Winter. Spray daily. Light place, no sun. High air-humidity and high temperature: 18-25°C (64-76°F). **Feeding:** Once a fortnight, in Summer only. **Propagation:** Cuttings under plastic (air layering). **Repotting:** Spring, in shallow pot.

FITTONIA argyroneura
(small leaves)
Nerve plant
Flowering season: None.
Care: Plenty of water in Summer, less in Winter. Spray daily. Light place, no sun. High air-humidity and high temperature: 18-25°C (65-78°F). **Feeding:** Once a fortnight. **Propagation:** Cuttings under plastic (air layering). **Repotting:** Spring in shallow pot.

FUCHSIA

Flowering season: Spring-Autumn. **Care:** In Summer planty, water well, in Winter sparingly. Light, airy place, no direct sunlight. Does better out-of-doors in Summer. High air-humidity, Winter temperature 6-10°C. **Feeding:** Once a fortnight during Summer. **Propagation:** Head and shoot cuttings in July/August. **Repotting:** Spring.

GARDENIA jasminoides
Cape jasmine

Flowering season: Spring, Summer, Autumn. **Care:** Plenty of soft, luke-warm water when in flower, at other times, not too much water. Spray regularly. Light, warm, sunny place. Very high air-humidity. Temperature: 16-22°C. **Feeding:** Once a fortnight when in flower. **Propagation:** Cuttings in Spring, under plastic.

GLORIOSA rothschildiana

Flowering season: Late Summer. **Care:** Keep well moist, spray frequently when in flower. Light, sunny place. When plant has finished flowering, store bulb in a dry spot for several months. High air-humidity whilst in flower. Temperature: 20-28° C. **Feeding:** Once a fortnight whilst in flower. **Propagation:** Young bulbs. **Re-potting:** Early Spring.

GUZMANIA 'Amaranth'

Flowering season: Winter. **Care:** In Summer, plenty of soft, luke-warm water, also in sepal. Less water in Winter and not in sepal. Spray frequently. Light, warm place, no sun. Very high air-humidity. Temperature: 18-22°C. **Feeding:** Once a fortnight whilst in flower. **Propagation:** Re-pot young plants. **Re-potting:** Unnecessary.

GUZMANIA dissitiflora

Flowering season: Winter. **Care:** In Summer, plenty of soft, luke-warm water, also in sepal. Less water in Winter and not in sepal. Spray frequently. Light, warm place, no sun. Very high air-humidity. Temperature: 18-22°C. **Feeding:** Once a fortnight whilst in flower. **Propagation:** Re-pot young plants. **Re-potting:** Unnecessary.

GUZMANIA 'Marlebeca'

Flowering season: Winter. **Care:** In Summer, plenty of soft luke-warm water, also in sepal. Less water in Winter and not in sepal. Spray frequently. Light, warm place, no sun. Very high air-humidity. Temperature: min. 18°C max. 22°C (64-72°F). **Feeding:** Once a fortnight whilst in flower. **Propagation:** Re-pot young plants. **Re-potting:** Unnecessary.

GUZMANIA 'Mini Exodus'

Flowering season: Winter. **Care:** In Summer, plenty of soft, luke-warm water, also in sepal. Less water in Winter and not in sepal. Spray frequently. Light, warm place, no sun. Very high air-humidity. Temperature: min. 18°C max. 22°C (64-72°F). **Feeding:** Once a fortnight whilst in flower. **Propagation:** Re-pot young plants. **Re-potting:** Unnecessary.

GUZMANIA minor
Orange star

Flowering season: Winter. **Care:** In Summer, plenty of soft, luke-warm water, also in sepal. Less water in Winter and not in sepal. Spray frequently. Light, warm place, no sun. Very high air-humidity. Temperature: min. 18°C max. 22°C (64-72°F). **Feeding:** Once a fortnight whilst in flower. **Propagation:** Re-pot young plants. **Re-potting:** Unnecessary.

GYNURA procumbens
Purple passion plant

Flowering season: Autumn (seldom). **Care:** Plenty of water in Summer, less in Winter. Light, sunny place. Pinch out top from time to time. Normal air-humidity. Temperature: Summer above 20°C, Winter 15-18°C. **Feeding:** Once a month from April through November. **Propagation:** 10 cm cuttings in May/September. **Re-potting:** In Spring.

HEDERA canariensis
Canary Island ivy

Flowering season: None. **Care:** Not too much water, spray occasionally. Reasonably light place, no direct sunlight. Air-humidity: not too low. Temperature: 15-20°C in Winter approx. 12°C. **Feeding:** Once every two to three weeks during growing season. **Propagation:** Cuttings (10-15 cm). **Re-potting:** In Spring, if necessary.

HEDERA helix-hybr.

Flowering season: None. **Care:** not too much water, spray occasionally. Reasonably light place, no direct sunlight. Air-humidity: not too low. Temperature: 15-20°C in Winter approx. 12°C. **Feeding:** Once every two to three weeks during growing season. **Propagation:** Cuttings (10-15 cm). **Re-potting:** In Spring, if necessary.

HEDERA helix 'Glacier'

Flowering season: None. **Care:** Not to much water, spray occasionally. Reasonably light place, no direct sunlight. Air-humidity: not too low. Temperature: 15-20°C in Winter approx. 12°C. **Feeding:** Once every two to three weeks during growing season. **Propagation:** Cuttings (10-15 cm). **Re-potting:** In Spring, if necessary.

HEDERA (hanging plant)

Flowering season: None. **Care:** Not too much water, spray occasionally. Reasonably light place, no direct sunlight. Air-humidity: not too low. Temperature: 15-20°C in Winter approx. 12°C. **Feeding:** Once every two to three weeks during growing season. **Propagation:** Cuttings (10-15 cm). **Re-potting:** In Spring, if necessary.

HIBISCUS rosa-sinensis
Rose of China

Flowering season: Summer-Autumn. **Care:** Plenty of water and fresh air, spray frequently. Warm, light place, no direct sunlight. High air-humidity. Temperature: in Winter 12°C. **Feeding:** Once a week during flowering season. **Propagation:** Cuttings, 10-12 cm. **Re-potting:** In Spring, but only when absolutely necessary.

HIPPEASTRUM (Amaryllis)-
red
Amaryllis
Flowering season: Winter-
Spring. **Care:** Water sparingly until bud becomes visible.
Reasonably light-sunny
place, according to state of
growth. Low air-humidity.
Feeding: Once a week, also
after plant has finished
flowering. Oct. through Dec.
none. **Propagation:** Re-pot
young bulbs. **Re-potting:**
December-January.

HIPPEASTRUM (Amaryllis)-
pink
Amaryllis
Flowering season: Winter-
Spring. **Care:** Water sparingly until bud becomes visible.
Reasonably light-sunny
place, according to state of
growth. Low air-humidity.
Feeding: Once a week, also
after plant has finished
flowering. Oct. through Dec.
none. **Propagation:** Re-pot
young bulbs. **Re-potting:**
December-January.

HIPPEASTRUM (Amaryllis)-
white
Amaryllis
Flowering season: Winter-
Spring. **Care:** Water sparingly until bud becomes visible.
Reasonably light-sunny
place, according to state of
growth. Low air-humidity.
Feeding: Once a week, also
after plant has finished
flowering. Oct. through Dec.
none. **Propagation:** Re-pot
young bulbs. **Re-potting:**
December-January.

HIPPEASTRUM (Amaryllis)-
orange
Amaryllis
Flowering season: Winter-
Spring. **Care:** Water sparingly until bud becomes visible.
Reasonably light-sunny
place, according to state of
growth. Low air-humidity.
Feeding: Once a week, also
after plant has finished
flowering. Oct. through Dec.
none. **Propagation:** Re-pot
young bulbs. **Re-potting:**
December-January.

HIPPEASTRUM (Amaryllis)-
deep-red
Amaryllis
Flowering season: Winter-
Spring. **Care:** Water sparingly until bud becomes visible.
Reasonably light-sunny
place, according to state of
growth. Low air-humidity.
Feeding: Once a week, also
after plant has finished
flowering. Oct. through Dec.
none. **Propagation:** Re-pot
young bulbs. **Re-potting:**
December-January.

HIPPEASTRUM (Amaryllis)-
white/red, striped
Amaryllis
Flowering season: Winter-
Spring. **Care:** Water sparingly until bud becomes visible.
Reasonably light-sunny
place, according to state of
growth. Low air-humidity.
Feeding: Once a week, also
after plant has finished
flowering. Oct. through Dec.
none. **Propagation:** Re-pot
young bulbs. **Re-potting:**
December-January.

HOWEIA (Kentia) forsteriana

Flowering season: Old plants only. **Care:** Medium to large amount of water, spray frequently, sponge leaves. Light place, no direct sunlight. High air-humidity. Temperature: max. 22°C. **Feeding:** Once every two to three weeks during growing season. **Propagation:** Seeding (a professional job). **Re-potting:** Once every three years.

HOYA bella (hanging variety)
Miniature wax plant

Flowering season: Sometimes twice a year. **Care:** Plenty of water when in flower. Little or no water during rest period. Light place, no direct sunlight. Fairly high air-humidity. Temperature: Summer, above 15°C, Winter 12-15°C. **Feeding:** Once a fortnight during growing/flowering season. **Propagation:** Cuttings in peat-mould.

HOYA carnosa
(climbing variety)
Wax plant
Flowering season: Sometimes twice a year. **Care:** Plenty of water when flowering, spray frequently. Little to no water during rest period. Light place, no direct sunlight. Train over a hoop. Air-humidity: relatively high. Temperature: in Summer above 15°C, in Winter 10-12° C. **Feeding:** Once a fortnight. **Propagation:** Shoot cuttings in peat-mould.

HOYA micrantha

Flowering season: Sometimes twice a year. **Care:** Plenty of water when flowering, spray frequently. Little to no water during rest period. Light place, no direct sunlight. Train over a hoop. Air-humidity: relatively high. Temperature: in Summer above 15°C, in Winter 10-12° C. **Feeding:** Once a fortnight. **Propagation:** Shoot cuttings in peat-mould.

HOYA multiflora

Flowering season: Sometimes twice a year. **Care:** Plenty of water when flowering, spray frequently. Little to no water during rest period. Light place, no direct sunlight. Train over a hoop. Air-humidity: relatively high. Temperature: in Summer above 15°C, in Winter 10-12° C. **Feeding:** Once a fortnight. **Propagation:** Shoot cuttings in peat-mould.

HYDRANGEA
macrophylla-hybr.

Flowering season: Spring and early Summer. **Care:** Plenty of water. Prune back after flowering. Cool, reasonably light place, no sun. Can stand outside from beginning of June. Relatively low air-humidity. Temperature: 15-18°C, Autumn/ Winter 5-10°C. **Feeding:** Once a fortnight whilst in bloom. **Propagation:** Top shoot cuttings.

HYPOCYRTA glabra
Clog plant

Flowering season: Spring, Summer, Winter. **Care:** In Summer plenty, in Winter moderate amount of luke-warm water. Light to sunny place. Fairly high air-humidity. Temperature: Summer 16-18°C, Winter 10-15°C. **Feeding:** Once a fortnight whilst in flower. **Propagation:** 5 cm shoot cuttings. **Re-potting:** Spring, when necessary.

HYPOESTES taeniata
Polka dot plant

Flowering season: Summer. **Care:** Normal amount of water, less in Winter, spray frequently with luke-warm water. Very warm, light place, no direct sunlight or draught. Very high air-humidity. Temperature: 15-20°C **Feeding:** Not necessary. **Propagation:** Top shoots in hot-bed. **Re-potting:** In Spring, shallow pot.

JATROPHA podagrica

Flowering season: Summer, but only full-grown plants. **Care:** Normal amount of water during Summer, keep roots moist. Once leaves have fallen off, very little or no water. Normal air-humidity. Temperature: not too low. **Feeding:** Unnecessary. **Propagation:** Seeding. **Re-potting:** April.

KALANCHOE
Blossfeldiana-hybr.
Flaming Katy
Flowering season: Any season, if handled under short-day method. **Care:** Water sparingly. Cool airy place, no direct sunlight. Prune back after flowering. Air-humidity: not too low. Winter temperature: 10-15°C. **Feeding:** Once a month, in Summer. **Propagation:** Top and/or leaf cuttings, seeding, baby plants. **Re-potting:** Young plants only.

MARANTA leuconeura 'Fascinator'
Prayer plant
Flowering season: None (blossom insignificant). **Care:** Moderate light, no sun. Spray daily, even in Winter. Use luke-warm rain water by preference. Temperature: 16-22°C, in Winter approx. 12-16°C. **Feeding:** In Summer once a fortnight. **Propagation:** By slipping young shoots, in Spring or Summer. **Re-potting:** Spring.

MEDINILLA magnifica

Flowering season: Spring-Summer. **Care:** Plenty of water whilst growing/flowering, less during Winter. Spray. Light, warm, damp place. Air-humidity: very high. Temperature: Summer 18-24°C, Winter approx. 15°C. **Feeding:** Once a fortnight whilst in flower. **Propagation:** Cuttings in Jan./Feb. in hot-bed. **Re-potting:** Young plants.

MONSTERA deliciosa
('Philodendron')
Cheese plant
Flowering season: older plants only. **Care:** luke-warm water daily in growing season; spray, sponge leaves weekly. Warm, light place, no hot sunlight. High air-humidity. Temperature: Winter 12-20°C. **Feeding:** once a fortnight March-Nov. **Propagation:** cuttings under plastic in warm-bed. **Re-potting:** Spring.

NEOREGELIA carolinae
Meyendorfii
Flowering season: flowers negligible. **Care:** plenty of water in growing season, less in Winter. Keep roots moist. Light place, no direct sunlight. High air-humidity. Temperature: 23°C. In Winter min. 15°C. **Feeding:** once a fortnight during growing season. **Propagation:** young shoot cuttings. **Re-potting:** every Spring in shallow pots.

NEOREGELIA carolinae
'Perfecta tricolor'
Flowering season: flowers negligible. **Care:** plenty of water in growing season, less in Winter, spray regularly. Light place, no direct sunlight. High air-humidity. Temperature: 23°C. In Winter min. 15°C. **Feeding:** once a fortnight during growing season. **Propagation:** young shoot cuttings. **Re-potting:** every Spring in shallow pots.

NEOREGELIA carolinae
'Flandria'
Flowering season: flowers negligible. **Care:** plenty of water in growing season, less in Winter, spray regularly. Light place, no direct sunlight. Temperature: 23°C. In Winter min. 15°C. **Feeding:** once a fortnight during growing season. **Propagation:** young shoot cuttings. **Re-potting:** every Spring in shallow pots.

NEPHROLEPSIS exaltata
Boston fern
Flowering season: none. **Care:** Plenty of soft water in Summer, less in Winter, roots mustn't dry out, spray frequently. Moderately light, not too warm place, no sun. High air-humidity. Temperature: 16-18°C (60-65°F). **Feeding:** Once a fortnight in growing season. **Propagation:** root division, planting runners. **Re-potting:** Spring, when necessary.

NERIUM oleander
Oleander
Flowering season: Summer. **Care:** plenty of water in Summer, spray frequently. Light, sunny place, fresh air, can go into the garden in Summer. Less water in Winter. Low air-humidity. Temperature 18-25°C Winter 5-10°C. **Feeding:** weekly during growing/flowering season. **Propagation:** top cuttings in peat-mould under plastic.

NERTERA granadensis
Bead plant

Flowering season: Spring, berries later. **Care:** moderate amount of water in saucer, shallow pot. Light place, fresh air, no direct sunlight. Normal air-humidity. Temperature: 16°C (60°F), Winter: 10-12°C (50-55°F). **Feeding:** once a week when in flower. **Propagation:** root division. **Re-potting:** Spring.

NIAM niamensis
(impatiens)

Flowering season: Spring-Summer. **Care:** plenty of luke-warm water whilst flowering, spray regularly. Light place, no sun. Temperature: 15-18° (60-65°F), Winter approx. 10°C (40°F). **Feeding:** once a fortnight. **Propagation:** Top-shoots. **Re-potting:** Spring, if necessary.

OPUNTIA + CYLINDRO-PUNTIA

Flowering season: only out-of-doors. **Care:** Water normally whilst growing, very little from October on. Warm, light, very sunny place. Low air-humidity. Temperature: approx. 20°C, in Winter 5-7°C. **Feeding:** once a fortnight whilst growing. **Propagation:** cuttings, beginning of May. **Re-potting:** Spring, if necessary.

PACHYPODIUM lamerii

Flowering season: none. **Care:** water moderately when growing (May-Aug.) little in Winter. Permanent, light place, no direct sunlight. Spray regularly and sponge leaves. High, deep pot. High air-humidity. Normal temperature, not below 15° C. **Feeding:** once a fortnight during growing season. **Propagation:** seeding (difficult). **Re-potting:** April.

PACHYSTACHYS lutea
Lollypop plant

Flowering season: Spring-Winter. **Care:** plenty of water whilst growing and flowering, spray. Permanent, light, airy place, no sun. High air-humidity. Normal temperature: Winter abt. 15°C (60°F). **Feeding:** twice a fortnight, not during Winter. **Propagation:** cuttings under plastic in warm bed. **Re-potting:** Spring, if necessary.

PALMA cyclanthus
Palm

Flowering season: none. **Care:** plenty of water in Spring/Summer, little in Winter. Spray regularly and sponge leaves. Tall, deep pot. Light place, no direct sunlight. Temperature: normal, not below 15°C. **Feeding:** once a fortnight during growing season. **Propagation:** seeding (difficult). **Re-potting:** April.

PAPHIOPEDILUM-hybr.

Flowering season: according to variety. **Care:** plenty of (rain) water when in flower. Spray until flowers open. Window sill facing east, no sun. High air-humidity. Temperature abt. 18°C (65°F), in Winter min. 12°C (54°F). **Feeding:** once a fortnight whilst in flower. **Propagation:** root division. **Re-potting:** Spring, after plant has finished flowering.

PASSIFLORA coerulea
Passion vine

Flowering season: Summer-Autumn. **Care:** Lots of water whilst flowering. Sunny place, fresh air. Does well out-of-doors in Summer. Normal air-humidity. Winter temperature: 5-10°C (40-50°F). **Feeding:** once a fortnight whilst flowering. **Propagation:** young shoot cuttings in warm bed. **Re-potting:** Spring.

PELARGONIUM-hybr.

Flowering season: Summer. **Care:** moderate amount of water; no stagnant water. Light, warm place, no very hot sunlight, fresh air. High air-humidity. Summer temperature: 17-20°C. Keep indoors over Winter at 5-10° C. **Feeding:** once a fortnight during flowering season. **Propagation:** cuttings Aug.-Sept. **Re-potting:** Spring-Summer.

PELLAEA rotundifolia
Button fern

Flowering season: none. **Care:** moderate amount of water, spray. Reasonably light place, no sun. Keep roots moist. Air-humidity: not too low. Temperature: 18-20°C (64-68°F). In Winter: min. 10-12°C (50-53°F). **Feeding:** once a month. **Propagation:** root separation. **Re-potting:** Spring, in wide, shallow pot.

PENTAS lanceolata
Egyptian star cluster

Flowering season: Autumn-Winter, sometimes till Spring. **Care:** Moderate amount of water, spray regularly. High air-humidity. Fresh air, no draughts. Light place, no sun. Temperature: 15-20°C. Pinch out regularly. **Feeding:** each three weeks during flowering season. **Propagation:** cuttings. **Re-potting:** After flowering season, if necessary.

PEPEROMIA obtisufolia
'Variegata'

Flowering season: according to variety. **Care:** moderate amount of water (island), spray regularly. Light, warm place, no sun. High air-humidity. Temperature 18-20°C (64-68°F). **Feeding:** twice monthly in Summer. **Propagation:** top shoot or leaf cuttings in Spring. **Re-potting:** only when necessary.

PHILODENDRON
'Emerald Queen'

Flowering season: none.
Care: normal amount of
water, spray regularly.
Location depends on variety,
not too much light. High air-
humidity. Temperature:
16-24°C (60-75°F), variegated and hairy varieties: not
below 18°C (65°F). **Feeding:**
once a month during
Summer. **Propagation:**
cuttings. **Re-potting:** Spring,
if necessary.

PHILODENDRON laciniatum

Flowering season: none.
Care: normal amount of
water, spray regularly.
Location depends on variety,
not too much light. High air-
humidity. Temperature:
16-24°C (60-75°F), variegated and hairy varieties: not
below 18°C (65°F). **Feeding:**
once a month during
Summer. **Propagation:**
cuttings. **Re-potting:** Spring,
if necessary.

PHILODENDRON pandurae
forme

Flowering season: none.
Care: normal amount of
water, spray regularly.
Location depends on variety,
not too much light. High air-
humidity. Temperature:
16-24°C (60-75°F), variegated and hairy varieties: not
below 18°C (65°F). **Feeding:**
once a month during
Summer. **Propagation:**
cuttings. **Re-potting:** Spring,
if necessary.

PHILODENDRON 'Red
duchess'

Flowering season: none.
Care: normal amount of
water, spray regularly.
Location depends on variety,
not too much light. High air-
humidity. Temperature:
16-24°C, variegated and
hairy varieties: not below 18°
C. **Feeding:** once a month
during Summer. **Propaga-
tion:** cuttings. **Re-potting:**
Spring, if necessary.

PHILODENDRON 'Red
emerald'

Flowering season: none.
Care: normal amount of
water, spray regularly.
Location depends on variety,
not too much light. High air-
humidity. Temperature:
16-24°C, variegated and
hairy varieties: not below 18°
C. **Feeding:** once a month
during Summer. **Propaga-
tion:** cuttings. **Re-potting:**
Spring, if necessary.

PHILODENDRON scandens
Sweetheart plant

Flowering season: none.
Care: normal amount of
water, spray regularly.
Location depends on variety,
not too much light. High air-
humidity. Temperature:
16-24°C (60-75°F), variegated and hairy varieties: not
below 18°C (65°F). **Feeding:**
once a month during
Summer. **Propagation:**
cuttings. **Re-potting:** Spring,
if necessary.

PHLEBODIUM
Haresfoot fern

Flowering season: none.
Care: moderate to plenty of
soft water in Summer, little
in Winter. Keep roots moist
(island). Not too light a
place, spray regularly. High
air-humidity. Winter temperature: 16-18°C (60-65°F).
Feeding: once a fortnight
during growing season.
Propagation: root division.
Re-potting: Spring, when
necessary.

PHOENIX canariensis
Date palm

Flowering season: none.
Care: Summer plenty.
Winter little water. Spray.
Warm, light sunny place.
Winter: cool place. Average
air-humidity. Temperature:
Winter 5-10°C. **Feeding:**
once a week during Summer.
Re-potting: planting the
stones, root division.
Propagation: only if roots
grow through hole at bottom
of pot.

PILEA

Flowering season: none.
Care: in Summer, normal to
plenty of water. Do not
spray. Less water in Winter.
Warm, sunny place. Can go
outside in Summer. High air-
humidity. Indoor tempera-
ture in Winter: min. 10°C.
Feeding: once a fortnight
during Spring/Summer.
Propagation: cuttings in
water. **Re-potting:** Spring,
when necessary.

PISONIA umbellifera
'Variegata'

Flowering season: none.
Care: plenty of water (island)
during growing season,
thereafter, less. Keep roots
damp. Light, rather warm
place, no direct sunlight.
Very high air-humidity.
Winter temperature: 18-20°C
(64-68°F). **Feeding:** very
little. **Propagation:** head and
stem cuttings in warmbed.
Re-potting: Spring.

PLATYCERIUM bifurcatum
Staghorn fern

Flowering season: none.
Care: as potted plant: normal
amount of water; as hanging
plant: submerge pot in luke-
warm water twice a week.
Never spray or sponge. High
air-humidity, no draught.
Temperature: 18-22°C.
Feeding: once every three
weeks in Summer. **Propagation:** root separation. **Re-
potting:** older plants.

PRIMULA obconica-hybr.

Flowering season: Winter +
Spring. **Care:** medium
amount of soft water.
Remove dead-heads.
Reasonably warm place, no
sun. Normal air-humidity.
Temperature: 10-15°C. In
Winter: min. 10°C. This plant
can cause skin irritation.
Feeding: once a week whilst
in flower. **Propagation:**
seeding. **Re-potting:**
perennials only.

PTERIS

Flowering season: none.
Care: plenty of water during growing season. Spray. Keep roots moist. Moderately light place, no sun. High air-humidity. Moderate temperature, in Winter min. 10-12°C. **Feeding:** once a fortnight during growing season. **Propagation:** root separation, sowing. **Re-potting:** Spring.

RHAPHIDOPHORA aurea
Devil's ivy

Flowering season: none.
Care: water whenever potting mixture is dry, Spray regularly. Warm, light place, no sun. Fairly high air-humidity. Room temperature, Winter min. 12°C (53° F). **Feeding:** once a fortnight during growing season. **Propagation:** top and stem cuttings. **Re-potting:** Spring, if necessary: wide, shallow pot.

RHIPSALIDOPSIS gaertneri
Easter cactus

Flowering season: Spring.
Care: plenty of soft water during growing/flowering season. Spray. Little water during rest period. Reasonably light place, no sun. High air-humidity. Winter temperature: 10-12°C. Once buds set: 15-18°C. **Feeding:** once a month during growing season. **Propagation:** leaf cuttings from fully grown specimens.

RHOEO spathacea 'Vittata'
Moses in a cradle

Flowering season: unimportant. **Care:** plenty of water (island) in Summer, little water in Winter. Spray regularly. In Summer, shady spot, in Winter, light place, no sun. High air-humidity. Temperature: 16-20°C (60-68°F). **Feeding:** once a week in Summer. **Propagation:** side shoot cuttings, seeding. **Re-potting:** Spring, if necessary.

RHOICISSUS 'Ellen Danica'

Flowering season: older plants only. **Care:** not too much water, keep roots well moist. Spray. Moderately light place, no sun. High air-humidity. Temperature: cool to moderately warm, in Winter, min. 12°C (53°F). **Feeding:** once a month. **Propagation:** axillary cuttings in warm bed. **Re-potting:** regularly, after pruning.

SAINTPAULIA-hybr.
African violet

Flowering season: several times a year. **Care:** normal, soft, luke-warm water in saucer. Moderately light place, no sun. High air-humidity. Temperature: 16-22°C (60-70°F). **Feeding:** once a fortnight when in flower. **Propagation:** leaf cuttings. **Re-potting:** infrequently, shallow pot.

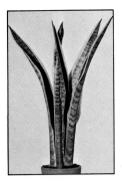

SANSEVIERIA trifasciata
'Laurentii'
Mother in law's tongue
Flowering season: Spring.
Care: moderate amount of
luke-warm water, very little
in Winter. Do not water in
leaf calyx. Light, warm place,
no direct sunlight. Low air-
humidity. Temperature: 16-
20°C. **Feeding:** once a
fortnight during Summer.
Propagation: root separation, leaf cuttings in
warmbed. **Re-potting:** only
when necessary.

SAXIFRAGA 'Tricolor'
Mother of thousands

Flowering season: early
Summer. **Care:** keep
moderately moist. Light, not
too warm place, no sun.
Fairly high air-humidity.
Room-temperature, in
Winter, min. 10°C (50°F).
Feeding: once a fortnight
during growing season.
Propagation: re-pot see-
dlings. **Re-potting:** Spring,
shallow pot.

SCHEFFLERA venulosa
Umbrella tree

Flowering season: none.
Care: plenty of water during
growing season, less in
Winter. Spray. Light,
moderately warm place, no
direct sun, fresh air. Normal
air-humidity. Temperature:
12-17°C (53-62°F). **Feeding:**
once a week during growing
season. **Propagation:**
seeding under plastic in
warm bed. **Re-potting:**
Spring.

SCHEFFLERA venulosa
'Compacta'

Flowering season: none.
Care: plenty of water during
growing season, less in
Winter. Spray. Light,
moderately warm place, no
direct sun, fresh air. Normal
air-humidity. Temperature:
12-17°C (53-62°F). **Feeding:**
once a week during growing
season. **Propagation:**
seeding under plastic in
warmbed. **Re-potting:**
Spring.

SCHEFFLERA venulosa
'Greengold'

Flowering season: none.
Care: plenty of water during
growing season, less in
Winter. Spray. Light,
moderately warm place, no
direct sun, fresh air. Normal
air-humidity. Temperature:
12-17°C (53-62°F). **Feeding:**
once a week during growing
season. **Propagation:**
seeding under plastic in
warmbed. **Re-potting:**
Spring.

SCHEFFLERA 'Henriette'

Flowering season: none.
Care: plenty of water during
growing season, less in
Winter. Spray. Light,
moderately warm place, no
direct sun, fresh air. Normal
air-humidity. Temperature:
12-17°C (53-62°F). **Feeding:**
once a week during growing
season. **Propagation:**
seeding under plastic in
warmbed. **Re-potting:**
Spring.

SCHEFFLERA 'Renate'

Flowering season: none.
Care: plenty of water during growing season, less in Winter. Spray. Light, moderately warm place, no direct sun, fresh air. Normal air-humidity. Temperature: 12-17°C (53-62°F). **Feeding:** once a week during growing season. **Propagation:** seeding under plastic in warmbed. **Re-potting:** Spring.

SCIRPUS cernuus

Flowering season: none.
Care: a great deal of water in saucer. Spray frequently. Light, not too warm place, no sun. Very high air-humidity. Temperature: 10-15°C (50-60°F). **Feeding:** once a month. **Propagation:** root separation or seeding. **Re-potting:** Spring, when necessary.

SCUTELLARIA 'Moniniana'

Flowering season: Summer.
Care: Light place, direct sunlight from time to time does not harm. Rather high air-humidity, moderate amount of water, spray regularly. Fresh air, in Summer plant can stand outside. **Feeding:** once a fortnight whilst growing. **Propagation:** root separation, in Spring. **Re-potting:** Spring, if necessary.

SEAFORTHIA (Chrysalido carpus) lutescens

Flowering season: none.
Care: plenty of water in Spring/Summer, little in Winter. Spray regularly and sponge leaves. Tall, deep pot. Light place, no direct sunlight. Temperature: normal, not below 15°C. **Feeding:** once a fortnight during growing season. **Propagation:** seeding (difficult). **Re-potting:** April.

SELAGINELLA

Flowering season: none.
Care: Plenty of soft, luke-warm water, spray frequent-ly, keep roots moist. Light, warm place, no sun. High air-humidity. Room-temperature, in Winter min. 15°C (60°F). **Feeding:** once a fortnight. **Propagation:** shoot cuttings under plastic. **Re-potting:** when necessary.

SELENICEREUS

Flowering season: in Summer (1 night). **Care:** plenty of water in Summer, keep rather dry in Winter. Warm, light place, no direct sun. High air-humidity. Winter min. 10°C (50°F). **Feeding:** cactus manure once in a while during Summer. **Propagation:** stem cuttings. **Re-potting:** Spring, when necessary.

SENECIO rowleyanus

Flowering season: indifferent. **Care:** moderate amount of water during growing season, keep fairly dry during resting period, shallow pot. Light, sunny place. Room temperature, cool in Winter. **Feeding:** seldom. **Propagation:** 5 cm cuttings. **Re-potting:** if the peas shrivel up.

SINNINGIA-hybr.

Flowering season: Spring/ Summer. **Care:** plenty of soft, luke-warm water when in flower (island), warm, light place, no sun. High air-humidity. Temperature: 20°C (68°F). In Winter, min. 6°C (42°F). **Feeding:** once a week whilst flowering. **Propagation:** runners, leaf cuttings. **Re-potting:** re-pot bulb in February.

SOLANUM capsicastrum
Winter cherry

Flowering season: Summer, berries later. **Care:** plenty of water whilst in flower (island), thereafter less, spray berries. Prune in Spring and Autumn. Light, sunny place. High air-humidity. Winter temperature: 8-10°C. **Feeding:** once a week whilst in flower. **Propagation:** seeding under plastic. **Re-potting:** Spring, in small pot.

SOLEIROLIA soleirolii
(Helxine)
Baby's tears
Flowering season: insignificant. **Care:** moderate amount of water in saucer, keep roots moist. Light place but no sun, fresh air. Fairly high air-humidity. Temperature: not too high. **Feeding:** once a month during growing season. **Propagation:** root separation. **Re-potting:** in Spring, if necessary.

SPARMANNIA africana
House lime

Flowering season: Winter, Jan.-March. **Care:** Light place, no direct sunlight. Can stand outside in Summer (sheltered spot, no sun). Especially whilst growing and flowering plenty of water, spray regularly. **Feeding:** Spring and Summer, once a fortnight. **Propagation:** Top- or side-shoots. **Re-potting:** after flowering.

SPATHIPHYLLUM
Peace lily

Flowering season: Differing. **Care:** Light place, no sun (in Winter sun is permitted). High air-humidity, plenty of luke-warm water, spray regularly. Temperature: in Winter at least 15°C. **Feeding:** Jan.-Oct., once a fortnight. **Re-potting:** root-separation or seeding. Spring. **Re-potting:** Each Spring.

STEPHANOTIS floribunda
Madagascar jasmine

Flowering season: Summer/
Autumn. **Care:** plenty of
water during growing and
flowering period (island).
Spray regularly, also during
Winter. Light place, no direct
sun. High air-humidity.
Temperature: 12-18°C. In
Winter, min. 12°C. **Feeding:**
once a fortnight during
growing season. **Propagation:** cuttings. **Re-potting:**
young plants in Spring.

STREPTOCARPUS-hybr.
Cape primula

Flowering season: Summer.
Care: plenty of soft, luke-
warm water (island). Light
place, no direct sunlight,
fresh air. In Winter, dryer
and cooler. High air-
humidity. Temperature abt.
18°C (65°F), in Winter min.
6°C (40°F). **Feeding:** none.
Propagation: leaf cuttings,
seeding. **Re-potting:** every
Spring.

SUCCULENTAE

Flowering season: accord-
ing to variety. **Care:** an
occasional, generous dose of
soft water during the
Summer, in Winter, less.
Warm, sunny place, fresh
air, fairly low air-humidity.
Temperature: warm in
Summer, in Winter abt. 8°C.
Feeding: none, or very little.
Propagation: top, sideshoot
or leaf cuttings. **Re-potting:**
April/May.

SYNGONIUM
Goosefoot plant

Flowering season: none.
Care: Air-humidity and heat
are more important than
light. Hanging- and climbing-
plant. Plenty of luke-warm
water, spray regularly. High
air-humidity. Temperature:
at least 15°C. **Feeding:** once
a fortnight, except in Winter.
Propagation: Top-shoots or
stem cuttings. **Re-potting:**
Each year after growing
season.

THUNBERGIA alara
Black eyed Suzie

Flowering season: early
Summer-Autumn. **Care:**
Plenty of water during
growing/flowering season,
less in Winter. Light, sunny
place, fresh air. Air-
humidity: not to low.
Temperature: 18-20°C. In
Winter 10°C. **Feeding:** once
a week during growing
season. **Propagation:**
seeding. **Re-potting:**
(annual).

TILLANDSIA flabellata

Flowering season: May and
June. **Care:** plenty of soft
water when in flower. Spray
frequently. Light place, no
direct sunlight. Rather high
air-humidity. Room temperature, min. 13°C. **Feeding:**
once a week whilst in
flower, thereafter once a
fortnight. **Propagation:** re-
pot offsprings after flowering
season; also root separation.

TILLANDSIA leiboldiana

Flowering season: May and June. **Care:** plenty of soft, luke-warm water when in flower. Spray frequently. Light place, no direct sunlight. Rather high air-humidity. Room-temperature, min. 13°C. **Feeding:** once a week whilst in flower, thereafter once a fortnight. **Propagation:** re-pot offsprings after flowering season; also root separation.

TRADESCANTIA 'Rochfords Silver' **Wandering Jew**
Flowering season: Summer, but insignificant. **Care:** water regularly in Summer, less in Winter, keep roots moist. Needs plenty of light, but no direct sun. Normal air-humidity. Temperature: cool, in Winter min. 10°C. **Feeding:** once a fortnight during growing season. **Propagation:** top-shoots and root division. **Re-potting:** Spring.

VRIESEA splendens **Flaming sword**

Flowering season: dependent on variety. **Care:** plenty of soft, luke-warm water in leaf calyx during Summer. In Winter, water sparingly over earth. Spray regularly. Light warm place with constant temperature, no direct sunlight. **Feeding:** once a fortnight during Summer. **Propagation:** re-pot young suckers at end of flowering season. **Re-potting:** Spring.

VRIESEA poelmannii

Flowering season: dependent on variety. **Care:** plenty of soft, luke-warm water in leaf calyx during Summer. In Winter, water sparingly over earth. Keep roots moist. Spray regularly. Light warm place with constant temperature, no direct sunlight. **Feeding:** once a fortnight during Summer. **Propagation:** re-pot young suckers at end of flowering season. **Re-potting:** Spring.

VRIESEA 'Vulkana'

Flowering season: dependent on variety. **Care:** plenty of soft, luke-warm water in leaf calyx during Summer. In Winter, water sparingly over earth. Keep roots moist. Spray regularly. Light warm place with constant temperature, no direct sunlight. **Feeding:** once a fortnight during Summer. **Propagation:** re-pot young suckers at end of flowering season. **Re-potting:** Spring.

YUCCA elephantipes

Flowering season: older plants only, in Summer. **Care:** plenty of water in Summer, less in Winter. Sponge leaves. Light, warm place, can go outside during Summer. Normal to low air-humidity. Winter temperature: 6-7°C (42-45°F). **Feeding:** once a week, in Summer only. **Propagation:** seeding, root division, re-pot young suckers. **Re-potting:** Spring, when necessary.

SOME OTHER SORTS

CHRYSANTHEMUM
indicum-hybr.

Chrysanthemum is an
abundantly flowering house
plant. Growers control the
day length of the plant to
induce year round flowering.
If you plant a Chrysanthemum that has finished
flowering outside in May, it
will grow to a shrub with a
height of approx. 1 metre,
flowering in Autumn (when
the days are getting shorter).

SENECIO cruentus-hybr.

The flowering season of this
house plant depends on the
growers method; it usually
begins in January, and ends
in May. Besides a house
plant, Senecio is also a
decorative feature in your
window box. Take care,
however, that the plants do
not have to suffer damage
caused by ground-frost at
night.

CODONANTHE crassifolia

A hanging-plant, flowering in
late Summer or Autumn with
small but very beautiful white
flowers. Give a moderate
amount of water each few
days and spray regularly;
take good care that the plant
gets all the light it needs, but
avoid direct sunlight.

GERBERA-hybr.

Gerbera has been well-
known as a cut-flower for
many years. It became
particularly popular because
of its soft colours. The
Gerbera is very attractive
both as a house and garden
plant. Spray regularly and
give a moderate amount of
water. The speed at which
the flower-buds grow is a
pleasure for every amateur
botanist.

BLECHNUM gibbum
(Lomaria)

Like all palms, this plant
needs plenty of water whilst
growing as well as regular
spraying with luke-warm
water. It is useful to sponge
the leaves now and then.
Place Blechnum in a deep pot
and avoid direct sunlight and
draughts.

FERNS (mixed)

Although ferns will never
bear flowers, as house plants
they are surprisingly graceful
because of their varying leaf-
shapes and tones. They
require a high air and
compost humidity and it is
useful to spray regularly. As
their natural surroundings
are always shady, it is
recommended to find a
shady place for the ferns in
your room too.

PLANT ARRANGEMENT

Human beings are creatures of habit. Most of us have our own way of doing things and this applies even to the way in which we arrange the plants in our homes. Normally they will be placed upon a window-sill or in front of a window. There are, however, plenty of other possibilities.

The window has many advantages, the main one of which is that the plant gets plenty of light. But there are also disadvantages. For one thing it is difficult to protect your plants from direct sunlight. For another there is the problem that comes in Winter when, with the room heating on, the plant gets warmth from one side and cold through the window pane on the other.

If you do want to stand your plant on the window sill all the year round don't make the mistake of placing too many tall ones with dense foliage there. This will tend to make the room too dark and the plants standing further from the window will be starved of light.

Be careful also not to create too stiff an effect e.g. by placing several *Sansevierias* in a row – the vertical growth of this plant is better complemented by lower plants with more variety in shape.

This leads us naturally on to the

question of the combination and arrangement of plants. We don't want to overload you with advice on this matter because you will want to make up your own mind on how and where to arrange your plants to suit the effect you desire. It is, however, important to take the requirements of the individual plants into consideration. Bear in mind the 'big three' factors of light, humidity and temperature.

In order to provide the ideal condition for your plants you should combine arrangements of those plants which have similar requirements from this point of view. The care suggestions on pages 34-73 will be of help where this is concerned. Once you have taken these factors into consideration, the rest is up to you. Always remember, though, that plants hate draughts, they should be within easy reach for

Evergreens with a touch of colour provided by the variegated leaves of the Begonia rex. Note: tall at the rear short at the front.

More privacy can be provided on either side of a glass dividing wall in home or office by a house plant screen.

daily care and should not be in a place where regular contact is made with them. Brushing past them regularly turns the leaves brown. When arranging plants always put the taller ones at the back and the smaller ones at the front and try to achieve a good contrast in colours and leaf shape. The shape, colour and style of the plant pots is also important.

As long as it's not cold or blowing a gale give your plants a breath of air in the garden now and again. A Summer shower? Let them enjoy it. You will notice almost immediately how much good this does your plants.

Watering: You wouldn't like it if someone poured a bucket of cold water over your feet so why do it to your plants. They much prefer luke-warm water.

Cacti and **succulents** can take plenty of sun. The only exceptions are the leafy varieties which must be protected from direct sunlight as you would protect any other house plant. All cacti need water from time to time. In Winter they need a cool, dry place.

Watering Cans: These are available in all shapes and sizes but despite this some people still prefer to use an old kettle. Find yourself a watering can which will hold several litres of water to avoid repeated trips.

Geranium cuttings are best taken in August but since they are very easy-going plants you can plant cuttings from them at practically any time of the growing season and can usually count on success.

Flowerpots come in all shapes and sizes and you will choose the ones which you like best but beware of excessively colourful ones. They can tend to detract from the plants themselves.

Plants in baskets are fine so long as you line the basket with thick plastic so that it is completely watertight. The effect of plants in baskets can be very decorative especially if you leave the plants inside their own pots and hang the baskets in groups at different heights, for instance, on a wall.

Dirty pots. Once your flowerpots become empty always clean them very thoroughly. It makes no difference whether they are plastic or earthenware, always give them a good scrub with hot water with a generous pinch of soda in it and rinse thoroughly. Dirty pots are a favourite breeding place for plant-disease bacteria.

Primulas have the reputation of causing itchy skin and some people appear to be allergic to them. This is especially true of the *Primula obconica* though other varieties are less likely to cause trouble.

When the **heating** is on the air humidity drops dramatically. In humans this can cause head-aches and a prickly feeling in the eyes and you can bet that your plants also suffer from this dry-ness. Help them by spraying and providing water for evapo-ration.

If you must **move plants** about from one room to another with a different temperature do it grad-ually so that your plants have a chance to acclimatize. Sudden changes of temperature, as we have already said, can cause great damage to your plants. Also bear this in mind when you bring home new plants. It is better not to bring them indoors from the cool air straight into a very warm living room.

Chalk spots on leaves are caused by spraying with hard, chalk-containing water. They are unsightly but the remedy is simple: spray or sponge them with one of the many leaf-shine products available in spray or tube form.

Bonsai is the Japanese name for dwarf-tree. This one is a mini-conifer. Although these plants are primarily destined for the garden, they also make good house plants. They need a light, warm place and enough water.

Water-Islands. Since the great majority of plants need to be kept damp, plant-lovers are very fussy about watering and spraying and quite rightly so. Most pots do especially well if

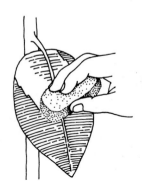

A bulb on gravel. Here we have a Paperwhite, a variety of Narcissus which you can plant on a gravel bed at the end of September/beginning of October. Place a layer of coarse gravel on the bottom of a glass bowl and add water to a level just below the bottom of the bulb. Paperwhite bulbs do not need to be kept in the dark and they must not be kept in too warm a place. Within a few weeks your bulb should flower. If the flowers show signs of drying out they are standing in too warm a place.

you provide a special system for water evaporation from below the pot. You can do this by means of a so-called 'island'. Turn a plate or saucer upside down and place it in a shallow bowl. Place the flowerpot on top of the overturned plate or saucer and fill the bowl with water to a level just below the bottom of the flowerpot. The water in the lower plate or saucer can then evaporate all around the plant. Remember to keep adding water when necessary.

Azaleas need plenty of water. At least once a week place your plant in a bucket of luke-warm water, to a level just above the soil. **Cyclamen** also thrive on this treatment, except that you musn't let the top section of the corm get wet. Both plants like a reasonably cool place to stand at night.

RE-POTTING

Re-potting is not difficult as long as you observe some basic rules... Start by putting some stones at the bottom of your pot. Place both the stones and the pot in water for at least 24 hours so that the pot is completely saturated. If you have a plastic pot this is obviously not necessary. Always make it a rule to re-pot your plants into the same type of pot – in other words a plant which grew in a plastic pot should be transferred into another plastic pot. Once the pot is prepared remove the plant from its old pot but be very careful, you cannot be rough or impatient when doing this work. Spread the fingers of one hand over the root crown and the earth surrounding the plant. Pick up the pot in your other hand and turn it upside down. Now tap the edge of the pot against a hard surface. The roots will usually come loose but if they don't do not pull at them, this can seriously damage the plant. When the roots are stubborn it is better to break the pot – the broken pieces can always be used to line the bottom of plant boxes. When your plant is out of its old pot, shake the roots gently to remove as much of the old earth as possible, then place the plant into its new pot. Fill up with new soil around the edges. If your plant needs a larger pot

This plant badly needs re-potting: the roots are growing through the hole at the bottom.

First, clean the pot thoroughly; place a broken piece of pot over the hole and put about 3 cm of potting compost into the pot.

Place the fingers of one hand over the root crown. Work the plant loose gently, don't pull.

Shake the old earth off the roots, place the plant in its new pot and fill with fresh potting compost.

select one which is one to two sizes larger, this will be quite sufficient. Once the plant is in place press the earth down gently all around it and make a watering groove with your thumb all around the edge of the pot. Do not fill the pot to a height more than one or two centimetres below the top edge. Potting compost can be purchased from most garden centres and shops or you can make up a mixture yourself by using two parts of manure to one of gritty sand. Another mixture can be made from peat-mould, artificial manure and trace elements. Some plants require a generous quantity of sphagnum moss and for orchids this is essential. Other plants such as *Alamanda, Aloe* and *Oleander* need a little loam or clay in their soil. Place your newly re-potted plants in a position which is light and warm but not in direct sunlight, they will need a little time to recover from the treatment.

The Asplenium nidus like loose, airy compost.

PRUNING

The plants in your living room have to put up with conditions which are very different from those they encounter in their wild state. They thrive despite artificial heat from the fireplace or central heating and they have to put up with air pollution as well – no-one asks house plants whether they mind if you smoke! They have to resist draughts and rapid temperature fluctuations when doors are opened. Despite all this they still manage to survive, often for many years, under these unnatural conditions and maintain their natural cycle. Most of our house plants stop growing during the Winter.

The rest period ends in February and, just like plants in the garden, they awake to a new growing season. When potting and re-potting our house plants it is important to bear in mind this natural cycle. It is best to tidy them up towards the end of February. Dead leaves and stems should be removed and plants which have grown a little

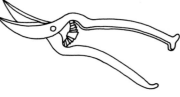

If you use a pruning knife, make sure it's very sharp.

When pruning, follow the gardeners' rule and prune after the plant has flowered. Instead of pruning, you can sometimes just snip off a few leaves or flowers.

wild should be pruned back into shape. Some plants may have outgrown their pots and need larger ones while the earth in other pots may have become undernourished.

Maintenance work must be carried out before the arrival of Spring. Whatever happens don't forget to prune. Some of your plants will have grown too tall, others in contrast will have grown too bushy. Careful pruning will give them back their natural shape. Also remove excessive side-shoots from your climbing plants.

Pruning needs careful thought — don't just rush into it. Take each branch between your fingers, check it well and decide how much needs to be pruned off. Don't prune all branches to the same length, but make sure that the plant retains its natural shape. Don't be afraid of removing too much growth, a few centimetres one way or the other won't make that much difference and it is sometimes necessary to be fairly radical. Prune off the pieces one by one and always just above a node or new side shoot. These prunings can also be used as cuttings (see page 86). It is a general rule that pruning never does the plant any harm as long as it is done properly. On the contrary, in fact, pruning gives the remaining growth a better chance to develop. Always remember, though, that a really sharp knife or pruning shears should be used. Pruning causes wounds and if sharp instruments are used they will heal quickly.

If there is a house plant you are particularly fond of why not try to grow another of the same kind yourself. It's well worth trying and if you are successful it will give you a tremendous feeling of satisfaction. Taking cuttings and seeing them develop into new and healthy plants is one of the most rewarding aspects of growing house plants. You can watch your plant develop from the tiny cutting which you have planted and tended into a full-grown, flowering specimen just as beautiful as the original.

In nurseries propagation by means of taking cuttings is now quite a science and the knowledge gained by the experts has helped to make the process far easier for the rest of us.

When is the best time to take cuttings? In their natural state plants bud and sprout at the end of the Winter so it follows that early Spring is the best time to take cuttings from the majority of house plants. Start your own little nursery during the second-half of February by taking cuttings from the pieces you prune off your plants while freshening them up after the Winter.

But how does one obtain cuttings? First of all you need to take a very sharp knife. Plants are living organisms and are therefore susceptible to infection. Reduce this risk by making the 'wound' you cause as

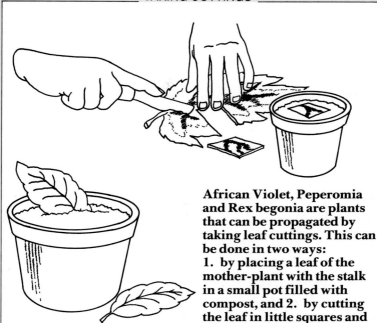

African Violet, Peperomia and Rex begonia are plants that can be propagated by taking leaf cuttings. This can be done in two ways: 1. by placing a leaf of the mother-plant with the stalk in a small pot filled with compost, and 2. by cutting the leaf in little squares and laying these on a mixture of peat dust and gritty sand.

clean and as straight as possible. The large majority of cuttings can be obtained from the pruned sections of the plant and the cutting you take should be 6-10 centimetres long, cut from just below a node. A node is the thickening on the stem from which develop buds and shoots. Next, dip the lower section of the cutting in water to a depth of one centimetre. Shake well to remove excess water and dip the cutting into rooting compound – a powdered, hormone product available at most garden centres and garden shops. This greatly increases the chances of success.

The cutting is now ready to plant. Prick a hole in potting compost with a thin twig and place the cutting carefully in the hole. A depth of 2 cm is sufficient.

Use a pot which is large enough to take about five cuttings and always remember – cuttings need plenty of room. Place the cuttings a few centimetres from the edge of the pot. As soon as they appear to have taken root you can transplant them gently into individual pots. Cuttings from certain plants (e.g. *Pelargonium*, all *cacti* and *succulent* plants) should be allowed to dry for a few hours before planting to prevent rotting. While on the subject of succulent plants, it is better to take cuttings from them a little later in the season, not usually before May.

Now your cuttings are neatly planted in their pot, give them a little water – but not too much – and then place a transparent bag over the top taking care not to touch the cuttings. This will protect them from draught and other dangers while still letting in enough light. Place the pot in a warm, light spot but not in direct sunlight and then leave them undisturbed. After three to four weeks check to see whether your work has been successful and to give the cuttings some water if they should need it. As soon as enough roots have grown to a sufficient length you can plant them carefully in individual pots. Among the plants which develop well in this manner are: *Aphelandra*, certain *Bego-*nia varieties (e.g. *Corallina, Maculata, Semperflorens), Cyperus, Fuchsia, Impatiens, Passiflora* and *Pilea cadierei.*

Other plants can be propagated by placing cuttings in a pot filled with water or by placing a leaf with stalk in potting compost or peat dust.

In this case the new plant grows from the base of the leaf, and this method works well with plants such as *Peperomia, Saint-paulia* and *Sinningia.*

When taking cuttings from *cacti* and *succulent plants* cut off a branch close to the main stem. The cutting should be left to dry for 24 hours before planting. If the plant has a milky sap, the open end of the cutting should be dipped in charcoal powder after you have cut it off. Remember – always use a sharp knife.

It is very easy to grow Geraniums (Pelargoniums) from cuttings and it is equally easy to propagate plants with trailing shoots, such as the Chlorophytum (right). Other propagation methods are illustrated on the opposite page: sowing, top shoot cuttings and stem and leaf cuttings. With love and patience, amazingly good results can be obtained.

ALL THE THINGS WHICH CAN GO WRONG

If leaves lose their colour this can often be caused by parasites – particularly by thrips. Remedy: wash the plant thoroughly and treat with a pyrethrum compound.

If the leaves look miserable and are misformed, check carefully for aphids. They extract sap from the leaves which then become undernourished. Remedy: wash leaves well and spray with a mixture of simple soap and spirit. See page 92.

Sticky leaves can be another symptom of plant pests. Same remedy as above.

White powder on the leaves: this indicates the presence of mildew. This is difficult to cure. There are special products available in the shops and spraying with sulphur sometimes helps.

Mealybugs: these are larvae which cover themselves with an unpleasant looking waxy fluff. Wash the plant thoroughly under heavy spray and then spray with a pyrethrum solution.

Thin, weak, leaf formation is usually the result of standing your plant in too dark a place or having too high a temperature in Winter. Remedy: prune off the offending stems or shoots in early Spring and in the meantime move the plant into more light and check the temperature.

If the leaves hang limply this can indicate two main causes – too little water, or too much water which can make the roots rot. Remedy: check the cause and improve the conditions accordingly.

If the leaves lose their markings the plant is not getting enough light.

If the leaves turn yellow you must give the plant more food – it is a sign of undernourishment.

If you find brown spots on the leaves the atmosphere in the room is too dry, though draught and too much bright sunlight can also cause this symptom.

If healthy leaves fall off you might have been giving the plant water which is too cold. The plant might also have been standing in a draught or have been subjected to dramatic fluctuations in temperature. It could also be too dry. Work out which is the case and remedy accordingly.

If blooms drop off without apparent reason then this, also, is a sign of abrupt temperature

It is temptingly simple to dispose of parasites by means of patent sprays, but remember that chemicals can also be dangerous (see pages 92-93).

fluctuations. It might also be that you have moved or turned the pot. Do not move or turn plants while they are in flower.
If the leaves develop brown edges the cause might be draught. You might also be constantly brushing up against it or the pot could be too small. Re-potting is really quite a simple matter, much easier than you think. See page 82.
If the root crown rots this means that the plant has been getting far too much water. It may also be too cold. Unfortunately there is little remedy for this but a prayer.
If, on the other hand, **the plant looks dried out** set it in a deep bowl of luke-warm water, hold the crown under water until no more air-bubbles escape and don't neglect it again!
If tiny white flies rise off the plant when you touch it spray with a solution of soap and spirit (see page 92) and repeat this every two or three days. These white flies are difficult to get rid of but, by spraying you prevent them laying eggs on the plant.
Spider mites – tiny webs on the undersides of the leaves – indicate that the plant is too dry. Remedy: increase air humidity and treat with a pyrethrum compound.

HOME REMEDIES FOR PESTS

Some old-fashioned remedies are more natural and are quite efficient at protecting our house plants against pests.

Stinging-nettle compost: it may not smell very nice but it is a pure, natural product which is both highly-efficient against pests and at feeding the leaves of your plants.

Spraying with stinging-nettle compost: this is wonderful for your plants. Collect some stinging-nettle leaves and stems and let them ferment in a bucket of water. After a few days strain off the water and add a little simple soap to it, to form the spray solution.

Soap and Spirit. This remedy is generations old and is still a good preventative and remedy for plant-pests and other enemies of your house plants – and your garden plants for that matter. Mix one litre of water with 25 grams of simple soap and 10cc of spirit. Put the solution in a plant mister and spray over your plants. Repeat regularly, the mixture cannot damage the plants.

Pyrethrum. This is an organic compound which is useful in combating aphids and thrips. It is made from the heads of a certain chrysanthemum variety and is available under various trade names: highly recommended.

Derris Powder (Also available in solution and spray form) is sometimes also called rotenon. This is also organic, originating from Derris roots, and is effective against aphids, thrips and white-fly.

Most old-fashioned remedies use organic compounds which are safe and natural but always remember that if you use chemical pest repellants these are far from harmless. Read

the instructions very carefully and be very cautious with their use.

As we have already explained, not every plant will grow equally well in any odd corner and the place you choose for your plant will exercise a strong influence over how it develops. The *Saintpaulia*, pictured below, is an example of a plant which develops yellow leaves if it gets too much direct sunlight. If you stand it in a draught you will soon see ugly spots on the leaves. If the stems grow limp, this is a sign of overwatering.

INDEX OF ENGLISH PLANT NAMES

Production: Inmerc BV, Wormer, the Netherlands.
Photography: Joop Valk; page 16 ABC Press.
Lithography: RCO, Velp.
Printing: BV Kunstdrukkerij Mercurius-Wormerveer.
© 1982 Mercbook International Ltd., Guernsey.
First published by Mercurius Horticultural Printers, 11 East Stockwell Street, Colchester, Essex. This edition published by Sphere Books Limited, London, 1984.